Literacy Coaching

Literacy Coaching

Transforming Teaching and
Learning with Digital Tools
and Technology

STEPHANIE AFFINITO

HEINEMANN
Portsmouth, NH

Heinemann

361 Hanover Street

Portsmouth, NH 03801–3912

www.heinemann.com

Offices and agents throughout the world

The author and publisher wish to thank those who have generously given permission to reprint borrowed material:

Figure 2.7: *What Makes Frequent Readers* Infographic from scholastic.com/readingreport. Copyright © 2017 by Scholastic Inc. Used by permission of Scholastic Inc.

(continued on page xii)

Library of Congress Cataloging-in-Publication Data

Names: Affinito, Stephanie, author.

Title: Literacy coaching : transforming teaching and learning with digital tools and technology / Stephanie Affinito.

Description: Portsmouth, NH : Heinemann, [2018] | Includes bibliographical references.

Identifiers: LCCN 2017051940 | ISBN 9780325092744

Subjects: LCSH: Language arts teachers—In-service training. | Language arts.

| Literacy—Study and teaching. | Educational technology. | Teachers—Professional relationships.

Classification: LCC LB2844.1.R4 A44 2018 | DDC 372.6—dc23

LC record available at https://lccn.loc.gov/2017051940

Editor: Holly Kim Price

Production: Victoria Merecki

Cover design: Suzanne Heiser

Cover image: © Getty Images/chatchaisurakram

Text design: Susan Godel

Typesetter: Shawn Girsberger

Author photo: Kemm Wilson

Manufacturing: Steve Bernier

Printed in the United States of America on acid-free paper

22 21 20 19 18 VP 1 2 3 4 5

To my husband, Joe, and my children, Hunter, Miranda, and Justice:
Thank you for believing in me before I believed in myself.

Contents

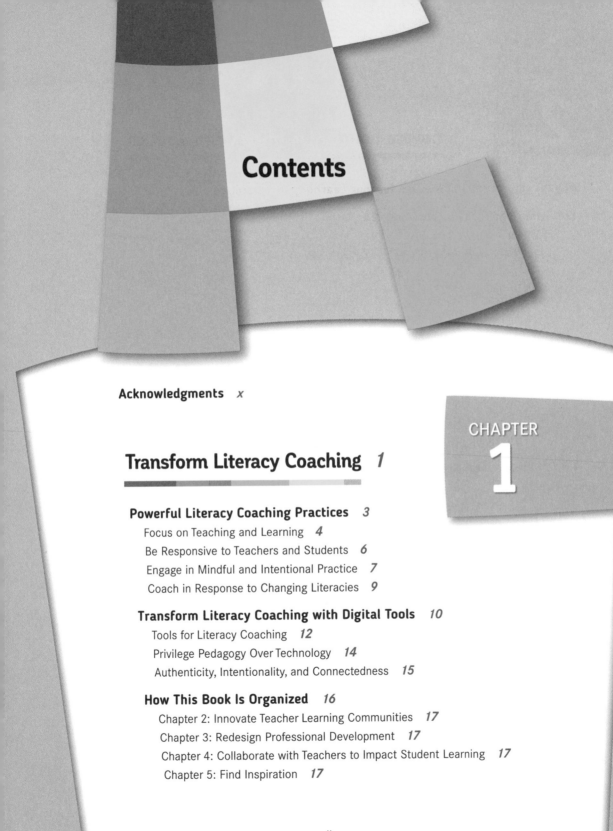

Acknowledgments

This book has been a journey of teaching, learning, coaching, and leading. As with any journey, this book would not be possible without the support, encouragement, and inspiration of many.

Above all, I thank my family. Thank you for the magical hours spent in the library, the countless trips to the bookstore, and the idea that I could one day be a writer too. To Joe, Hunter, Miranda, and Justice: Thank you for your support and encouragement to embark on my dream and share my ideas with the world. You have never doubted what I was capable of and celebrated with me every step of the way. I couldn't have done this without you.

I thank my colleagues in the Department of Literacy Teaching and Learning at the University at Albany, both past and present. I am honored to teach, work, and learn alongside each of you. I also thank my graduate students who push me to think and rethink what a supportive teacher learning environment looks like, both in person and online.

I would like to thank a few incredibly devoted #cyberPD members for their virtual inspiration that continues to this day: Cathy Mere, Laura Komos, Michelle Nero, Heidi Weber, Suz Porath, Kathleen Sokolowski, and Erika Victor. Your dedication to your own professional learning for the sake of your students is commendable.

Our collaborations through Voxer planted the seed idea that grew into this book. You each empowered me to be bold in my own learning and be open to the new possibilities that virtual collaboration could bring.

I am fortunate to have worked with an extraordinary Heinemann team, particularly my editor, Holly Kim Price. Holly, thank you for taking a risk on a new author and supporting me every step of the way. Your vision, insightful thinking, and constant encouragement are woven throughout every page of this book.

I would also like to acknowledge and thank the incredible literacy coaches and teachers I have the honor of learning and coaching with: Kristin Abrams, Nancy Cooke, Shelley Fenton, Logan Fisher, Ginny Mondschein, Maria Muldner, Krista Senatore, Kelly Toleman, Allison Walter, and many more. You continue to inspire me with the work you do each and every day. Thank you for sharing your professional lives with me and giving readers a glimpse into your coaching throughout this book.

As all educators do, I stand on the shoulders of the many literacy teachers, leaders, and researchers who came before me. They inspire me to better support teachers to ultimately impact student learning. Thank you to all the educators who continue to make the world a better place, one student at a time.

Transform Literacy Coaching

If you are reading this, I imagine that, like me, you have been on a journey. A journey that led you to literacy coaching and leadership and one that continues with celebrations, challenges, and plenty of bends in the road. My literacy coaching journey is built on stories: stories of success and stories of mistakes, peppered with varied stories of the many teachers and students I work with. Each story leaves a lasting impression on my work as a coach and paves the way for new learning. Recently, I hosted a series of professional development sessions for teachers who wanted to explore authentic reading response within their classroom. In those sessions, we returned to our roots as readers, carefully examined our practices, and set goals to renew reading instruction in our classrooms. We read books together, engaged in reading response, and added new digital tools to our instructional repertoire. Each session, we shared our attempts to transfer our learning to the classrooms. A few weeks after our sessions ended, Mary, one of the teachers, pulled me aside to share a heartfelt thank-you for our learning together. She explained our work together gave her the courage to let go of some old practices she was hanging onto in her classroom, giving our new ideas a chance to thrive. She told me about a student who was struggling greatly; after a few weeks of changed reading instruction, not only did this student's reading skills improve, but her motivation and willingness to engage was transformed. She now believed she was a reader. As Mary shared this story and credited our work together for this student's success, tears came to my eyes, and I was reminded just how important our work is not only to teachers but to students.

Not all our stories as literacy coaches are successes. Although my work as a coach had a clear and measurable effect on the students in Mary's classroom, this does not always happen as readily or as easily. I remember working with a kindergarten teacher to help strengthen her small-group reading instruction. I gave her information about what her guided reading lessons could look like, provided her with lesson templates and organizers (with a pretty font and icon that I knew she would appreciate!), modeled a lesson with students in her classroom, and talked about what her next steps might be. I was exhausted, but she was enthusiastic about our work and I looked forward to seeing the changes she would make. Imagine my disappointment when I visited her room a few weeks later to see her teaching her groups in the same way she always had, my resources pushed to the side of her kidney-shaped reading table. In that moment, I was reminded of what a challenging job coaching is, matching the right mix of support to teachers who might not be ready to change . . . yet.

I strongly believe that everything happens for a reason, good or bad, and each story has played a purposeful role in my professional journey. One particular story of mistakes set me on an unexpected but very eventful journey. A few years ago, I taught an online class designed to support teachers as they provided literacy instruction to students experiencing difficulty learning literacy. I was particularly proud of the online experiences I had designed for my courses: a carefully planned sequence of content, updated and powerful journal articles and professional readings, and ample opportunities for teachers to discuss their learning with peers. Yet the jarring, brutally honest feedback from a student stopped me in my tracks. I'll spare you the actual comments, but they went something like "very traditional online course," "need more face-to-face elements," "not in the twenty-first century," and a few more. I'll admit, this was a hard pill to swallow and I choked a bit on the comments. How could something so carefully constructed impact a learner in such a negative way? I could have passed it off as feedback from just one disgruntled student, but that is not in my nature, and I imagine many of you readers can relate. I realized that this student was not personally attacking me, but pushing me to reconsider what is possible for teaching and learning through technology. So, I began to reflect on my practices as a coach and online instructor (with a glass of red wine). I devoured literature on using technology to support teacher learning. I spent countless hours stumbling to learn new digital tools not simply to represent learning, but to transform it. I was on my own learning journey. It is this journey that I hope to share with you as you work to strengthen and transform your own coaching experiences supported through technology.

Powerful Literacy Coaching Practices

The International Literacy Association (2015) defines a literacy coach as a specialized literacy professional who primarily works with teachers and facilitates efforts to improve school literacy programs. Although seemingly a straightforward position, coaching is anything but linear. We are known by many names, work with both teachers and students, and juggle multiple responsibilities to improve classroom literacy practices and lead school reform efforts. On any given day, we might work with students, coach alongside teachers in their classrooms, analyze assessment data, and lead professional development sessions. We might also cover classrooms, tread through mounds of paperwork, shuttle through meetings, and juggle other obligations. What does your coaching position look like? Draw a quick sketch of what your role as a literacy coach looks like in your school. Based on Kaback's (2008) informal "draw-a-reader" assessment, drawing our practices gives us compelling insight into our work as literacy coaches. Don't worry about your drawing skills here, just give it a try. Figure 1.1 shows my own drawing and the drawing of one of the literacy coaches I work with.

Figure 1.1: *Draw-a-Literacy-Coach images from literacy coaches*

As you might expect, each of our drawings is different, representing the complex and varied roles we enact in our individual schools and districts. Yet, however unique, common threads bind us together in our efforts to support literacy teaching and learning. Typically, we work with teachers, although many of us also work with students to improve teaching practice. We lead school efforts to improve literacy instruction and student learning. Whether you are a literacy specialist who primarily works with students, a literacy coach who spends most of her time collaborating with teachers, or an administrator who oversees literacy curriculum and assessment in a district, we share a common bond of leading literacy. Some days might be balanced, some not. Some days might feel productive, some not. Each day, we are faced with decisions about how to spend our time as a literacy coach. How do we make these decisions? Some are personal choices based on our visions for the position. Some are mandated based on standards, curriculum and policy. Some are in response to teachers and their students' strengths and needs. Articulating our coaching philosophies—the what, how, and why of the work we do—is essential in leading the learning of others. Just as teaching philosophies and learning histories influence instructional actions within the classroom (Cole and Knowles 2000), our coaching philosophies guide our coaching actions as well (Dozier 2006). Based on my research and practice as a literacy coach and teacher educator, I have developed core beliefs about what literacy coaching is and how it transforms teacher learning.

Focus on Teaching and Learning

Literacy coaching relies on the assumption that coaching practices lead to changes in teacher knowledge and practice, which ultimately result in positive changes in student performance (Lockwood, McCombs, and Marsh 2010; Casey 2006; Dole 2004; International Reading Association [IRA] 2004; Lyons and Pinnell 2001; Moran 2007; Rodgers and Rodgers 2007; Toll 2005; Walpole and McKenna 2008). Literacy coaches cultivate the expertise of literacy teachers in multiple ways. The International Literacy Association's (2015) framework of coaching activities documents the ways we might work with teachers depending on the intensity of our coaching positions (see Figure 1.2).

Our coaching activities might range from building relationships with teachers to analyzing and changing teaching practice. Although any coaching activity has the potential to transform teaching and learning, the more intense collaborations with teachers are better apt to produce the greatest results. Yet, as coaches, we know all too well that higher levels of coaching and teacher engagement can be hard to reach for a variety of reasons. Here are some concrete steps you can take to ensure that your coaching continues moving teachers' instructional practices forward.

Level 1 (Informal; Building Relationships)	Level 2 (More Formal; Somewhat More Intense; Begin to Analyze Practice)	Level 3 (Formal; More Intense; Focus on Changing Practice)
• Conversations with colleagues (getting to know one another, identifying issues or needs, setting goals, initial problem solving) • Establishing schedules for meeting with groups of teachers and individuals • Establishing norms for collaboration and conversation • Developing and providing materials for/with colleagues • Developing curriculum with colleagues • Participating in professional development activities with colleagues (conferences, workshops) • Leading or participating in study groups • Assisting with assessment of students • Instructing students to learn about their strengths and needs • Coaching on the fly (unscheduled, brief meetings with teachers that provide opportunities for additional coaching)	• Conversations with individual colleagues about teaching, learning, and literacy (analyzing data, lessons) • Coplanning lessons • Revisiting norms for collaboration and conversation to make certain they facilitate group work • Holding team meetings (grade level, data, department) • Analyzing student work to assist teacher(s) in planning instruction • Analyzing and interpreting assessment data (helping teachers use results for instructional decision making) • Making presentations at professional development meetings • Assisting with online professional development	• Conversations focusing on coplanning, coteaching, and teaching dilemmas • Modeling and discussing lessons • Coteaching lessons • Visiting classrooms and providing feedback to teachers as part of the planning/observation/debrief cycle • Individual and group analysis of videotaped lessons of teachers • Engaging in lesson study with teachers • Participating in and leading professional learning communities • Providing support to teachers as a result of teacher performance evaluation outcomes • Involvement in efforts to improve school literacy programs • Facilitating school–community partnership work

Note: Two sources were used in the creation of this table: "Promoting Effective Literacy Instruction," by R. M. Bean (2004) and "Professional Learning as the Key to Linking Content and Literacy Instruction," by J. Ippolito (in Ippolito, Lawrence, and Zeller 2013).

International Literacy Association. (2015). The Multiple Roles of School-Based Specialized Literacy Professionals (Research Brief). Newark, DE: Rita Bean, Virginia Goatley, and Diane Kern. Retrieved from http://literacyworldwide.org/docs/default-source/where-we-stand/ila-literacy-professionals-research-brief .pdf. Reprinted with permission of the International Literacy Association.

Figure 1.2: *The International Literacy Association's (2015) framework of coaching activities of specialized literacy professionals*

1. Start with yourself. Take a moment to look at the chart and think about your coaching activities. What level do your coaching activities primarily fit into? Is one level more pronounced than the other? Are there places where your coaching could use a boost of intensity? Keep in mind that lower-level coaching activities are essential to build relationships with teachers that lead to more focused coaching work later on. If you are new to coaching or new to your building, it is essential that you focus on these level 1 activities to build a strong foundation for coaching.

2. Name a goal. Where do you want to make a change in your coaching to strengthen teaching and learning in your school? Do you want to better lead student data meetings and shift the culture from problem admiring to problem solving? Or do you want to carve out more time for modeling and coteaching lessons in the classroom? Make your goal concrete and post it in a place where you can refer to it often.

3. Identify challenges. What challenges might interfere with your more intense coaching work? Whose challenges are they? They might be your own unconscious discomfort or lack of confidence in working with teachers on such intense practices. Or, they might be organizational and school factors that hinder your coaching, such as scheduling issues or the inability to secure substitutes for coaching conferences and professional development.

4. Seek solutions. I once had an administrator say that we should never come to her with a problem unless we already had a possible solution. It changed the culture of the building and helped teachers think out of the box. Match every challenge you identified with a possible solution. Connect with other coaches to share and problem solve coaching challenges.

5. Take a risk. We often talk about literacy coaching in terms of the teachers' experiences—that it can be intimidating and even risky to put yourself out there and work with a coach to better your own teaching practices. But we never seem to talk about how risky that can feel as a coach as well. We might doubt our own abilities, feel insecure working with particular personalities, and choose lower-level coaching activities because they are simply more comfortable. But if we never take a risk, we never know what could have been and how many student lives we could have impacted if we had only given it a try. Start small, with interested teachers ready for more intense coaching, to build your confidence in a new coaching practice. Then slowly shift your coaching to higher levels of intensity with other teachers, based on your new coaching experiences and their readiness to engage.

6. Repeat. Over time, your own coaching skills grow in parallel with your teachers' instruction. Be sure to set new goals for yourself, and your teachers, as you gain newfound skills and confidence.

Be Responsive to Teachers and Students

To be effective, literacy coaches must be responsive to the needs of schools, teachers, and students (Dozier 2006; Ippolito 2008; Killion 2008; Rainville and Jones 2008; Smith 2009; Toll 2005) and cultivate a shared sense of inquiry into literacy instruction: "Responsive coaching is about learning—learning together, collaborating with colleagues, reflecting and creating spaces for inquiry" (Dozier 2006, 139). Coaches observe student engagement and response to instruction, collaborate to teach lessons and try new instructional techniques with teachers, and ensure that our support is varied and relevant for each teacher we work with. Literacy coaches help teachers become more analytical about their work, support teachers' application of knowledge, develop skills, polish technique, and deepen teachers' understanding (Lyons and Pinnell 2001). A literacy coach should not be viewed as an expert, but as someone quite knowledgeable about literacy instruction who grows alongside of the teachers she coaches. A few years back in a professional development session, a teacher posed a question to our group. Before other teachers could respond, one teacher interrupted and said, "Let the expert answer." I quickly discouraged this thinking and reminded teachers that although I may have had specialized literacy knowledge to share, they were experts on their students, not me, and that makes us learners on an equal playing field. Coaches and teachers must work alongside each other in pursuit of increased knowledge, strengthened instruction, and high levels of student performance.

As coaches, we must be flexible and respond to teachers and students in ways that meet their strengths, needs, and personal goals. We may have broad coaching goals, but the individual goals and activities we engage in with teachers are quite unique. For example, your school might be focusing on elevating small-group reading instruction as a building literacy goal. To support this work, you might provide whole-faculty professional development on small-group instruction, but your individual work with teachers will be varied. One teacher might focus on elevating her classroom management to allow for working with small groups of students, another might need to focus on using assessment results to guide his groupings, and yet another might be ready to create reading toolkits and demonstration notebooks. As coaches, we put our own assumptions aside and instead meet teachers where they are in their learning, even if it's not the starting place we would have hoped for or originally envisioned. As teachers grow and change, we alter our coaching plans and goals accordingly.

Engage in Mindful and Intentional Practice

Just as children learn something from our actions in the classroom, intentional or not, teachers also learn from our actions as literacy coaches. The professional development presentations, assessment meetings, coaching conversations, and every interaction in between send a message to teachers about literacy teaching, learning, and assessment. Therefore, each and every one of our actions needs to be a mindful, intentional model for the teachers we work with and must match the kinds of pedagogy we are advocating for in the classroom. We can't possibly expect teachers to implement a workshop model in their classroom by providing a brief, one-shot lecture-style session describing what a workshop classroom looks, feels, and sounds like. If we want teachers to act as facilitators for personalized learning, we have to engage them in an actual workshop approach: modeling minilessons, conferences, and share time; and giving teachers time to explore, ask questions, and collaborate with others.

Our literacy coaching practices must be clear and consistent models for literacy instruction. But our work cannot stop at modeling alone. In the classroom, we don't simply model what students should do without any additional guidance, scaffolding, or feedback. They need an explicit connection and an invitation to engage. We notice and name the specific strategies they are using as readers and writers and provide a concrete reminder of the ways they can help themselves as learners long after we leave. Teachers need and deserve the same care and attention. In your work with teachers:

1. Ensure that your coaching practices align with the pedagogy that you expect your teachers to transfer to their own classrooms. Are you encouraging teachers to take a workshop approach in their classroom? Ensure your professional development includes a whole-faculty lesson with explicit modeling, with time for teachers to engage in independent reflection and collaboration with others, and ends with a whole-faculty sharing. Are you sharing close reading practices to try in the classroom? Ensure that your session includes plenty of opportunities for teachers to read, annotate, and reflect together.

2. Notice and name the instructional moves you made as a coach as a model for your teachers. Did you survey teachers before beginning your session to drive your planning or session activities? Did you ask teachers to share their thinking and questions during the session using a virtual bulletin board or back channel? Specifically name the moves you made as a coach to facilitate teacher learning and talk about how those choices matter for teachers' learning as well as for their students' learning.

3. Extend an invitation for teachers to apply their own learning to their classrooms and back up the invitation with support. Move beyond the "You could try this in your classroom" comment at the end of a session and instead explicitly ask

teachers to have a go and connect to their classrooms. Offer coaching and re-sources along the way and follow up with personalized feedback.

4. When teachers try something new in their classrooms based on your work to-gether, celebrate and share. Together, build a culture of learning that permeates classroom walls and celebrates continued learning.

Coach in Response to Changing Literacies

Literacy today looks different than it did twenty years ago. In fact, literacy today looks different than it did one year ago! Education within the twenty-first century requires that we continually reimagine our definition of literacy and literacy instruction in the classroom. Literacy in today's times:

* changes our habits as readers (Bass and Sibberson 2015) and how readers share, discuss, and analyze text (Serafini and Youngs 2013; Serafini 2015)

* requires we participate in new mind-sets, identities, and practices (Vasquez 2010) and new social practices, skills, strategies, and dispositions (IRA 2009)

* is multitextual, multimodal, and multifaceted (IRA 2009)

* demands we use text, technology, and media critically and strategically for read-ing, composing, and learning (Muhtaris and Ziemke 2015).

Our classroom literacy instruction must shift and change in response to these new mind-sets and dispositions. The National Council for Teachers of English provides guidance on the kinds of teaching a twenty-first-century, global society demands. Today's classrooms must:

* Develop proficiency and fluency with the tools of technology;

* Build intentional cross-cultural connections and relationships with others so [as] to pose and solve problems collaboratively and strengthen independent thought;

* Design and share information for global communities to meet a variety of purposes;

* Manage, analyze, and synthesize multiple streams of simultaneous information;

＊ Create, critique, analyze, and evaluate multimedia texts;

＊ Attend to the ethical responsibilities required by these complex environments. (National Council for Teachers of English 2015)

Literacy teachers around the world are called on to amplify their instruction (Muhtaris and Ziemke 2015) with digital tools and other forms of technology to ensure students authentically create, communicate, collaborate, and learn together. We are asked to open our classroom doors, connect with other teachers and classrooms, and use technology in new, academic ways to strengthen creativity, learning, and motivation. We must provide new avenues for reading, writing, and discussing learning; provide access and ownership for all students; and build a community of learners that introduces students to worlds beyond their classroom walls, giving an authentic and connected audience for their literate work (Muhtaris and Ziemke 2015). Before teachers can imagine the ways technology can transform classroom instruction, they must first see the power and possibilities for such work in their own professional learning communities. To truly transform teacher learning, we must develop new practices that make use of the very tools and resources teachers might use in their own twenty-first-century classrooms. Literacy coaching offers particular promise for embedding these tools into our work.

Transform Literacy Coaching with Digital Tools

The Merriam-Webster Dictionary (2017) defines the word *transform* as "to change in composition or structure; to change the outward form or appearance of; to change in character or condition." Although the word might conjure up a grand vision of completely reimagining ourselves as literacy coaches, in reality, we transform our coaching all the time on different levels: in response to literacy policy and curriculum mandates, in response to new research and professional ideas, in response to teachers and students, and even in response to our own selves. Sometimes these transformations are welcomed, sometimes they are required, but each one has the potential to positively shift our practices. So why transform our literacy coaching with technology and digital tools? Technology has the ability to expand what is possible for coaching to make teacher learning more meaningful, relevant, and authentic. It can create global connections and expose teachers to worlds outside of their immediate classrooms. It has the potential to strengthen practice and teacher expertise through multimodal tools to help teachers become part of something larger than themselves.

We transform teacher learning through technology so teachers can integrate strengthened literacy practices into their classrooms. Through technology, teachers can collaborate, communicate, and learn in news ways they may not have yet experienced, meeting The International Society for Technology in Education (ISTE)'s (2016) standard of "tapping into technology's potential to amplify human capacity for collaboration, creativity and communication." You might think this work sounds like what a technology coach might do, but I am less focused on helping teachers implement digital tools into their classrooms and more focused on helping them use those tools to transform learning and professional practice. For example, fourth-grade teachers in upstate New York wanted to rethink the role reading logs play in their classrooms. During my time with them, I facilitated a session that began with a discussion about our current practices with reading logs and student responses. I shared compelling blog posts, graphics, and tweets to enrich the conversation. Using the name of the most recent book they had read, I asked teachers to fill out a traditional book log and add a digital Padlet tile to our Padlet wall: "Share a Book, Steal a Book" for comparison. Figure 1.3 outlines the session agenda.

My intent was to expand teachers' ideas of reading accountability in the classroom, and I used technology to help me accomplish that goal. My focus was on pedagogy made possible through multiple means of technology. My ultimate goal was not to have teachers use digital reading logs in the classroom, but to rethink their practices and make connections to their own classrooms.

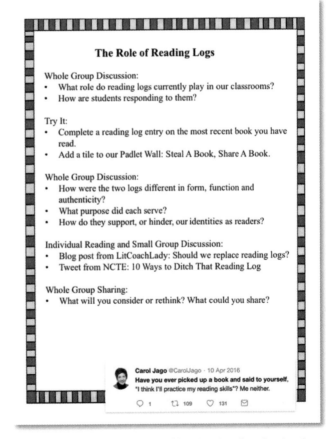

Figure 1.3: *Agenda for "The Role of Reading Logs" professional development session*

Literacy coaching with digital tools is not just coaching *with* digital tools, but coaching *through* digital tools, a critical distinction.

Tools for Literacy Coaching

Teaching tools help guide our teaching and our students' learning (Roberts and Beattie Roberts 2016). They help make our teaching clear, bring ideas and goals to life, and help learning stick. Literacy coaches have their own set of varied coaching tools to guide their coaching and learning. Think about all the coaching tools you use daily. Take a quick inventory and see what you discover. Just because technology is changing the way we work, learn, and play does not mean that the traditional coaching tools we rely on are obsolete. They still have an important role in our coaching. Here are some common, traditional literacy coaching tools:

* large pieces of chart paper or sticky notes

* notebooks and notepaper

* copies of needed papers and handouts

* in-person discussion

* printed books, lessons, and teaching artifacts.

Now, let's link them to the purpose that they serve in our coaching. Large pieces of chart paper or sticky notes encourage collaboration and represent the shared thinking of a group. Notebooks and note papers act as individual reflection tools to write down compelling thoughts and save important information for later use. Copies of handouts and papers, along with printed books, lessons, and teaching artifacts, ground the conversation in actual teaching and learning. Finally, in-person conversation is the medium in which we learn.

Fueled by interactions with others, we deepen our understanding, question our practices, and search for answers to our own questions. Even as the world around us becomes more and more advanced, we still rely on these old-fashioned, traditional coaching tools because our purpose of using them has remained the same. We still collaborate, we still grapple with big ideas, and we carefully analyze our teaching and assessment practices, yet technology has provided us with greater options for accomplishing these tasks. Options that can increase motivation and make teaching and learning more relevant, authentic, and immediate can transform our work. Let's look at how our traditional tools might expand and change into digital possibilities. Figure 1.4 offers a few ideas.

TRADITIONAL TOOL	DIGITAL TOOL
Large pieces of chart paper or sticky notes	Digital walls and bulletin boards
Notebooks and notepaper	Google Docs or other digital note-taking
Copies of needed papers and handouts	Digital curation of materials
In-person discussion	Digital and virtual conversations, tweets, and posts
Printed books, lessons, and teaching artifacts	Digital books, lessons, and teaching artifacts

Figure 1.4: *Traditional literacy coaching tools and digital transformations*

As we reimagine our coaching tools, we reimagine our coaching practices, which can shift, change, and expand through technology. Figure 1.5 provides a few examples to spark your thinking.

Literacy Coaching WITHOUT TECHNOLOGY	Literacy Coaching WITH/THROUGH TECHNOLOGY
Oral conversations with teachers throughout the school across the school day	Digital conversations with teachers across schools, days, and time zones
Create curriculum and lessons during after-school meetings and on curriculum days	Collaboratively create curriculum and lessons anytime and anywhere using collaborative documents
Meet to discuss a professional text in a book study	Participate in a digital community or use social media to discuss a professional text
Copy and share documents and lesson materials with other teachers	Curate documents and other materials digitally using digital bulletin boards
Discuss student learning in data meetings	Document and analyze student learning using digital tools and portfolios
Meet to discuss teaching interests and areas for inquiry into practice	Connect digitally and virtually to discuss teaching and practice
Create professional development sessions on a common topic	Create on-demand resources and tutorials for teachers to personalize their own learning

Figure 1.5: *Literacy coaching activities with and without technology*

As you can see, we do not abandon what we know works with our coaching in pursuit of using technology. Instead, we rely on what we know to be good coaching to connect with our teachers and cultivate their teaching expertise. We provide individual teachers with the tools they need to transform their own learning and develop in their own teaching journey. We must ensure that each tool we use has a specific purpose and has the potential to impact teacher learning. To truly transform our work, we must transform teachers' experiences, their minds, and their own mind-sets for learning. At times, more traditional tools will be more effective and at other times, digital tools may make the most impact.

Privilege Pedagogy Over Technology

As Muhtaris and Ziemke (2015) remind us, technology amplifies instruction. I would add that it amplifies instruction regardless of the quality of it. If you add technology to effective teaching, such as using digital devices in a well-established reading workshop, you end up with amplified effective teaching that changes students' ideas and perceptions of what reading is and could be. If you add technology to ineffective teaching, you end up with amplified ineffective teaching that simply reinforces students' single stories about themselves (Hale 2015). In her ISTE speech, Katharine Hale warns of the dangers of using technology in ways that do not expand students' ideas of what is possible for themselves, offering a powerful message for teachers.

Hale cautions against using apps that require students to answer questions in a quiz or game show fashion. In a traditional quiz setting, only the smartest, fastest kids get the answer first. With the technology, the activity might look more appealing and seem more effective, but essentially, the smartest and fastest students are still getting the answers first and the students who need more processing time and/or practice are still lagging behind. But now, results are showcased for all to see on a large screen. As Serafini (2015) reminds us, "If it doesn't help children as readers, it doesn't matter how shiny the new object is" (7). This same thinking applies to our work with teachers. If the tool does not support teacher learning, then why use it? We cannot add technology to our teaching and coaching just for the sake of adding technology to our teaching and coaching. If the tool does not provide any benefit to teachers' own learning and teaching, then don't use it. If the tool only provides a shinier object for teachers to teach in the

Scan the QR (Quick Response) code to view Katharine Hale's ISTE speech.
http://bit.ly/2BcBZ3Z

same old way, then abandon it. As literacy coaches, we must model careful, intentional, strategic, and authentic use of technology to help teachers imagine a classroom where technology is used to reimagine ourselves.

The ultimate validation for me as coach is to see the content and practices I share with teachers come to life in the classroom. I love receiving emails from teachers about something they tried, getting a text from a colleague celebrating a new practice, or seeing evidence of that work on social media or teacher community sites. It reminds me of the power we have as literacy leaders to impact teaching and learning on a larger scale. Our work with teachers changes their practice to impact students. Paired with digital tools, not only can we model literacy content and instructional practices to strengthen literacy instruction, but we can model intentional, authentic, and connected work with technology for students as well.

Once you have an idea of what you might hope to see in your teachers' classrooms, you can use that information to help shape the choices you make as a coach. If you know you need to shift the culture of student reading in the classroom and envision students using digital reading logs, you might start by creating opportunities for your teachers to experience the benefits in your coaching first. If you know you want to encourage teachers to differentiate instruction and allow for greater student choice, you

Scan the QR code to view the ISTE Standards for Educators.
http://bit.ly/2u8tRtL

might model how to do so with Google Forms and Surveys in your professional development. If you are interested in additional guidance to support technology innovations in the classroom, be sure to explore ISTE standards.

Authenticity, Intentionality, and Connectedness

In their work on creating engaged classrooms through the lens of digital reading, Bass and Sibberson (2015) offer three anchors to guide teachers' classroom instruction both with and without technology:

* Authenticity: keep reading a meaningful experience that extends beyond the classroom.

* Intentionality: make meaningful choices as readers.

* Connectedness: find and create connections between texts, readers, and experiences.

Although these anchors were originally intended to guide classroom literacy instruction, they can and should guide our literacy coaching as well, and they have been particularly powerful anchors for my own work. Here is how I make the parallel connection:

* Authenticity: keep teacher learning a meaningful experience that impacts and extends beyond the classroom. Digital tools can personalize teacher learning and help us own our teaching practices, reflect on our instruction, and learn through technology.

* Intentionality: make meaningful choices as teachers and instructional leaders. Provide teachers with choices in their own learning and the digital tools they use to meet their learning needs. We cannot make intentional decisions about our own teaching and learning unless we have multiple opportunities, contexts, and tools to choose among.

* Connectedness: find and create connections between texts, teachers, classrooms, and experiences. Digital tools can harness the power of sharing and community. They can engage and connect teachers across previously existing boundaries and bring us together as a community of learners both inside and outside our school walls.

Just as we privilege pedagogy in the classroom, we must do so as coaches. All too often, I have seen the focus placed on the tool over the learning. We have "appy-hours," "speed-apping" sessions, and more. Although they might seem appealing and introduce us to new digital tools, simply learning about and gaining fluency with digital tools is not enough. We must use them to strengthen teaching and learning. This starts with our coaching.

How This Book Is Organized

This first chapter introduced you to literacy coaching with digital tools and provided a framework for using technology to support teacher learning. In the remaining chapters, we explore the varied ways you can use technology to support teacher learning based on the common roles we take on as literacy coaches: building teacher learning communities, creating professional development experiences, and engaging in intentional classroom coaching.

Chapter 2: Innovate Teacher Learning Communities

In Chapter 2, I share how you might use technology to transform the learning community within your school. You will learn how to cultivate teachers' reading lives, create spaces for teacher learning, and cultivate your personal learning network alongside your teachers.

Chapter 3: Redesign Professional Development

In this chapter, I tackle professional development and offer numerous suggestions on how to use technology to differentiate your sessions, better engage teachers in their own learning, and curate useful instructional resources. You will learn about "flipped coaching" and imagine the possibilities for your own work.

Chapter 4: Collaborate with Teachers to Impact Student Learning

Intentional classroom coaching is at the heart of our work. In this chapter, you will reflect on your own coaching experiences and the decisions that drive your work in classrooms. I will share digital ways to plan, organize, and conference with teachers to elevate the level of literacy instruction in classrooms.

Chapter 5: Find Inspiration

In the final chapter of the book, I urge you to find inspiration for your continued journey. Inspiration can come in many forms: seeking out others, fueling your own professional learning, and staying connected. You will learn how to organize yourself for the journey ahead and take care of your professional digital footprint.

One of the teachers I work with has a coffee trivet that says "Life begins at the end of your comfort zone." As you read the chapters ahead, you might find that you feel a bit out of your comfort zone. Pause, take a deep breath, and realize this is actually a sign that you are ready to envision new possibilities for yourself, your teachers and their students. Throughout the chapters, you will find strategic "Launching Points" designed to help you pause, reflect, and identify a starting point for your work with technology. I have woven my stories of successes and mistakes throughout each chapter in the hope they will help you on your own journey to transform teacher learning as we coach in an ever-changing society. I also introduce you to the literacy coaches I work closely with to showcase their efforts and spark inspiration. You'll meet Shelley Fenton, Kristen Abrams, Krista Senatore, and other literacy coaches from New York kind enough to share their practices with you. Challenge yourself to learn something new, infuse your coaching with digital tools and technology, and empower teacher learning through innovative practices that inspire authentic change for the classroom as well.

Innovate Teacher Learning Communities

We all have defining moments in our careers: the moment we decided to become an educator; the moment we realized our instruction made a true impact on students; the moment we made the intentional decision to widen our reach and become a literacy coach. Recently, I had another defining moment in my career as a literacy educator. Jennifer Serravallo responded (Figure 2.1) to my post on The Reading Strategies Book Facebook Community:

Jennifer Serravallo This is INCREDIBLE. The finished product, the collaboration that went into creating them, and your generosity in sharing. Thank you on behalf of the hundreds of teachers who I'm sure will use these!

Unlike · Reply · 👍 22 · 13 hrs

Figure 2.1: *Comment from Jennifer Serravallo on The Reading and Writing Strategies Facebook Group*

Her post was in response to a collaborative product I shared with The Reading Strategies Book Facebook community page. A group of literacy coaches and I had worked over multiple sessions to collaboratively create a set of parent letters that connected to each of the reading goals in her book. I shared the finished products with the Facebook community along with a note about how critical the process of creating these letters was. I urged readers to use them as starting points for work within their own district, transforming teacher learning in the process.

Jennifer's response filled me with a sense of professional power. Our collaborative effort not only fueled our own enthusiasm and work, but by sharing it with the Facebook community, it had the potential to impact thousands of teachers, students, and their families. The power of collaboration, coupled with technology, had magnified our effort.

The power of peers is everywhere. Want to lose weight? Get a workout buddy. Want to learn to knit? Find a friend who does. Connection with others gives us power. It provides motivation and mental fuel for the work ahead, and widens our thinking. When we feel supported, when we have a tribe (Muhtaris and Ziemke 2015) of trusting supporters and mentors that inspire, we work differently. We expect success and feel comfortable taking risks to further our learning. We expect mistakes and welcome the opportunity to learn. Collaboration empowers teachers and changes the way we work in ways that could not happen if we were working alone. Together, we are more prepared to make instructional shifts that impact students.

In my years working with teachers, I have found the collaborative experiences—the ones that truly invite teachers to come together in a learning community in pursuit of a specific goal—are truly transformative. It is in these moments of collaboration and connection that we see our own learning and practice with new eyes, inspired by the synergy and energy that come with teamwork and collaboration.

Why It's Important to Innovate Teacher Learning Communities

The National Council for Teachers of English (NCTE) draws upon Skerrett's (2010) definition of teacher learning communities as "groups of teachers who continually inquire into their practice and, as a result, discover, create, and negotiate new meanings that improve their practice" (2010, 1). Essentially, a teacher learning community is a dedicated group of teachers who work collaboratively to pursue goals related to teaching and learning. These groups are teacher driven in the spirit of inquiry, not as a mandate from above, and they support teacher development and quality. According to NCTE (2010), teacher learning communities bridge the gap between research and practice, create spaces for addressing problems of practice, increase teacher retention, connect pedagogical practice with disciplinary/content area knowledge, foster transformative teaching, and improve student learning.

When we work together, we work smarter. If you have ever been a part of an effective learning community, you can feel the energy. Teachers are engaged and involved, and there is a buzz of conversation and a feeling of productivity in the air. Collaboration "extends the learning and thinking of everyone involved as coaches and teachers come to see teaching and learning with new eyes" (Dozier 2006, 35). Connecting and collaborating with others ignites our passion as teachers, maintains our motivation, and keeps our work intellectually challenging (Rami 2014), giving intention to our journey ahead.

To create true teacher learning communities, we must first build a foundation of trust, collegiality, and connectedness among teachers and school faculty. We must empower teachers to take control of their own learning through collaboration with others within an authentic learning community. We must vow to set a tone of mutual respect, positivity, and a shared goal to better our instruction for the sake of our students in our schools. Many teachers start the school year off creating a pact with their students to build a classroom community built on respect, hard work, collaboration with others, and a positive outlook on learning. These guiding principles create a solid foundation for successful learning experiences to come, and can guide our work with teachers as well. If we were to create a pact for learning with our teachers, it might look something like this:

1. Learning is never complete: We believe in lifelong learning and deserve the same innovative and effective support we provide to our students.

2. We work better together: We believe in collaboration with all faculty to push our thinking and further our learning.

3. Everyone plays a part: Each of us is important to our collaborative learning process. We all have a voice to contribute.

4. We learn from practice: We vow to open our classroom doors and invite connections with others.

5. We are in charge of our own journey: We deserve personalized learning experiences that are meaningful, authentic, and immediately applicable to our own classrooms.

Shared teacher learning in the digital age must be authentic, participatory, generative, and relevant to our teaching lives. Technology and digital tools can strengthen and expand a strong learning community to empower teacher learning. Figure 2.2 outlines the possible ways our traditional methods of building teacher learning communities might expand with the use of digital tools.

WITHOUT TECHNOLOGY, Coaches and Teachers . . .	WITH TECHNOLOGY, Coaches and Teachers . . .
Connect in informal settings throughout the school day (hallways, classroom doors, faculty rooms and meetings).	Connect through social media outlets and digital communities throughout the school day and beyond.
Share professional books, articles, and instructional ideas with each other.	Share, post, and contribute to online learning communities with teachers from all over the country, even the world.
Meet to discuss a professional text in a book study with colleagues.	Participate in a digital or virtual book study to discuss a professional text with teachers around the world.
Share books to read for pleasure with other interested teachers and readers.	Digitally share and archive our reading and writing lives through virtual communities.
Read and discuss literacy research and professional literature with colleagues.	Digitally access, annotate, and discuss literacy research and professional literature.
Participate in school-wide literacy events such as Get Caught Reading month.	Connect globally with other classrooms during virtual events such as the Global Read Aloud.

Figure 2.2: *Literacy coaching activities with and without technology*

Digital tools provide new ways of connecting with teachers, which leads to more collaborative and sustained work. Chances are you already use digital tools in your personal life. You might already be connected through multiple social media sites and browse blog posts and websites for ideas and inspiration for your next meal or home decorating project. You may already read e-books on your mobile device and take notes or jot reminders on an app. You might even connect with friends and family through video software, lessening the miles between you. These are real, authentic activities that connect us to others and are woven into the fabric of our lives. Why wouldn't we do the same in our literacy coaching? By using many of those same technologies, we can help teachers shift to using them in more academic ways for reading, writing, teaching, and learning, providing the same sense of connection and authenticity to our professional work. Figure 2.3 offers suggestions for using digital tools to reimagine how we create teacher learning communities.

TRADITIONAL TOOLS for Building Learning Communities	DIGITAL TOOLS for Building Learning Communities
Conversations and discussions	Posts, tweets, and digital conversations through digital and virtual communities
Printed personal books, articles, and resources	Digital texts, articles, and blog posts
Highlighters, sticky notes, and writing utensils for annotation and to facilitate discussion	Virtual sticky notes, infographics, and digital commenting tools
Colleagues and mentors to inspire and innovate instruction in the classroom	Researchers and professionals connected in digital and virtual contexts

Figure 2.3: *Traditional literacy coaching tools and digital transformations*

It is important to note that simply adding digital tools to our repertoire does not ensure increased collaboration and teacher learning. Transforming how we connect with teachers in the digital age means we collaborate, exchange ideas, and ultimately incorporate them into our instruction to impact student learning. The new voices, perspectives, ideas, and resources we encounter impact our teaching lives and provide opportunities for authentic renewal and growth.

Cultivate Reading and Learning

One weekday a few years ago, my son and I arrived late to school from an orthodontist appointment and were signing in at the office. His previous year's teacher walked by and stopped to give him a hug and say a quick hello. She turned and asked him, "So, Hunter, what have you been reading lately?" As he quickly answered her, I stood there in disbelief. She did not ask "How have you been?" or "How is the fifth grade going?" or even "What have you been up to?" Instead, her first eight words were, "So, Hunter, what have you been reading lately?" With those eight little words, she inspired both of us to reconnect with our reading lives and share them with her, inviting us into her community of reading and learning. If we create a community where authentic reading, writing, and learning are celebrated among teachers as well as students, we can change the entire landscape for literacy learning in a school.

Before we were teachers, we were readers—readers who understand the power reading has to change our lives from the new characters we meet, the new places we visit, and the new lessons we learn. As readers, we believe:

✳ Reading should be enjoyable and not portrayed as work.

✳ All readers should have time to read books they choose and that matter to them.

✳ Readers choose books based on interest, not just reading levels.

✳ Readers share books in authentic ways with others and build a community of readers.

✳ Reading does not mean answering comprehension questions or taking a quiz.

✳ We do not read to practice our reading skills, but to be changed by what we read.

I am sure that you could add to this list of beliefs and I encourage you to create your own reading bill of rights for the teachers and students you work with. Often, the many curriculum mandates, required assessments, and new initiatives take our time and attention away from what really matters, but our coaching can remind teachers of what is truly important. What do you know at your core about what reading really is and how it should be cultivated in the classroom? Chances are, your list includes some of the previous ideas and rests on the idea that we are all readers. As literacy coaches, we help teachers ensure real reading and writing experiences for their students by inviting them into a strong community of readers and writers as teachers. Teachers must be avid, wide readers and writers themselves to be effective and inspiring reading and writing teachers. As a coach, your actions can motivate and inspire teachers to carve out time for the reading and writing they know and love:

✳ Give book talks for both personal and professional texts.

✳ Create a free little library for your teachers to indulge in.

✳ Immerse teachers in reading by weaving references to books into your daily interactions.

✳ Share new titles and book recommendations often.

✳ Announce author birthdays along with teacher and student birthdays during morning announcements.

* Have book release parties for newly published children's, adult, and professional books.

* Create book clubs based on personal, not just professional, books.

* Encourage teachers to take part in local reading initiatives through the local library or bookstore.

There are multiple ways to use digital tools to reunite with your inner reader and cultivate a culture of literacy and literacy learning in your school. You might use digital tools to share your reading and writing lives; connect teachers to new professional ideas, research, and texts; and participate in local and global events to harness the power of reading.

Share Your Reading Lives

All the books I have read for pleasure in the past few years have come from the recommendations of others: from friends, from colleagues, and lately, from my children. In my travels, I have seen free little libraries on school grounds, shelves of "give-and-take" books in school faculty rooms and have even seen stacks of books and magazines in school restrooms. When books abound and a genuine buzz of talk and camaraderie surrounds them, readers find a way to them. Digital tools offer particular promise for archiving and sharing our reading and writing lives in real, meaningful, and authentic ways.

Goodreads is a social platform that allows readers to connect with other readers. You can share the books you are reading, find book recommendations, and discuss your reading with others. I was first introduced to Goodreads through my collaborative literacy coach group in upstate New York. As we met one summer day to discuss the books we were reading, I realized that some teachers were not writing down titles; instead they were adding them to their "Want to Read" stack on Goodreads. Intrigued by this new reading community, I created my own account and quickly followed suit, documenting books I recently read and creating a want-to-read shelf based on our conversations. The power in a tool like Goodreads is the ability to connect with other readers. It is one thing to document our reading for ourselves, but it is quite another to share our reading lives with others. By sharing and connecting in public ways, we acknowledge our status as a reader and invite connections with others based on our reading habits, interests, and inquiries. I admit, I need reminders to keep my profile up-to-date, but when I do, I am always amazed at the genuine reading community that awaits me. I encourage you to take some time to browse the Goodreads site and see for yourself. Start by posting the books you are currently reading and find a few that you hope to read. Once you have established your account, reach out to other readers and teachers. Connect with friends and teachers already on Goodreads and invite others to follow your lead. If you want to provide the same kinds of experiences for your students, consider exploring Bookopolis and BiblioNasium. Both are social reading platforms created specifically for students to share their reading lives with friends and family.

BE A TECHSPERT

BEGINNING

TECH TOOL

GOODREADS: *A site for readers and book recommendations*
WEBSITE: *www.goodreads.com*
COST: *Free!*
TECHSPERT LEVEL: *Great for beginning tech users*

Other tools can also help us archive and share our reading lives. Padlet is a virtual wall where people can add content (thoughts, images, videos, or documents) on a common topic easily and instantly to curate materials, organize thinking, and share ideas with others.

BE A TECHSPERT

BEGINNING

TECH TOOL

PADLET: *A virtual bulletin board*
WEBSITE: *https://padlet.com*
COST: *Free! Premium plans vary.*
TECHSPERT LEVEL: *Great for beginning tech users*

You can easily create a Padlet wall to share the books you are reading with your teachers in just a few quick steps. Title your Padlet 'What I'm Reading' and add tiles that showcase a book title, short description, and publishers' link. Figure 2.4 offers a view of a portion of my Padlet reading wall. Teachers can visit your Padlet wall for book recommendations and can even comment on your selections to offer their own ideas and suggestions.

Figure 2.4: *A screenshot of my "What I'm Reading" Padlet wall*

Once teachers see the power in such a practice, they can begin archiving their classroom reading lives as well. Teachers can create class Padlet walls to showcase the read-aloud of the day and even add a rating or student comments. Imagine how powerful it would be to scroll down the list of books read throughout the year! Teachers, students, and even parents can rejoice in the reading together. When we capitalize on the natural social interactions around books, we begin to create a powerful community of teachers who are readers. When teachers see firsthand the power in (and ease of using!) a tool like Padlet, they will see how it will also benefit their students.

> **LAUNCHING POINT** ✳
>
> *Create a "What I'm Reading" Padlet wall to share with your teachers. Log onto www.padlet.com or download the app to your digital device. Create a username and click the +Make a Padlet icon. Choose your title, background image, and format and save. Double-click on your Padlet wall and create your first tile. Title it with the title and author of the book you are reading and write a quick summary or teaser for teachers. Link to the website where teachers could find out more or even purchase the text. Be sure to allow for commenting so teachers can let you know what they think of your selections! Want to share? Tweet your link to @AffinitoLit to share with other readers!*

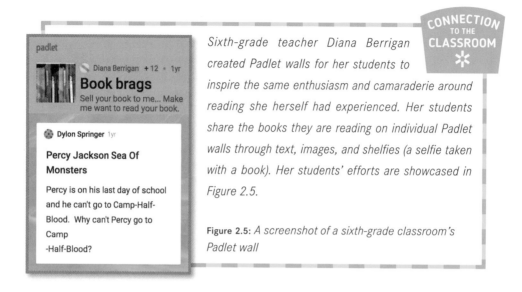

Sixth-grade teacher Diana Berrigan created Padlet walls for her students to inspire the same enthusiasm and camaraderie around reading she herself had experienced. Her students share the books they are reading on individual Padlet walls through text, images, and shelfies (a selfie taken with a book). Her students' efforts are showcased in Figure 2.5.

Figure 2.5: *A screenshot of a sixth-grade classroom's Padlet wall*

Foster Professional Reading with Infographics

For our coaching to be relevant, we must keep up-to-date on the latest research, professional literature, and literacy happenings that could potentially and positively impact the classroom and student learning. We read widely, browse literacy websites and blogs, and learn new ideas through conferences and professional events. Figure 2.6 provides multiple resources to remain current in our field.

It can be challenging to engage teachers in wide professional learning, given their incredibly busy lives in the classroom, yet technology and digital tools can innovate our practices. At the click of a button, the tap of a mouse, or the scan of a code, we can provide teachers with access to new research and ideas.

Information graphics, or infographics, are visual representations of information, data, or knowledge designed to present information quickly and clearly in an attractive format. Infographics are designed to share summaries of research, convey important data and statistics, represent learning from a project or activity, or simply invite wonder and curiosity for further reading and reflection.

I tend to use infographics in two ways: to jump-start conversation in professional development based on current research and to capture the main themes of a professional text to spark further

RESOURCES FOR RESEARCH AND PRACTICE

Literacy Journals

The Reading Teacher	http://ila.onlinelibrary.wiley.com/hub/journal/10.1002/(ISSN)1936-2714/
Journal of Adolescent & Adult Literacy	http://ila.onlinelibrary.wiley.com/hub/journal/10.1002/(ISSN)1936-2706/
Reading Research Quarterly	http://ila.onlinelibrary.wiley.com/hub/journal/10.1002/(ISSN)1936-2722/
Journal of Literacy Research	http://journals.sagepub.com/home/jlr

Professional Organizations

International Literacy Association	https://literacyworldwide.org
National Council for Teachers of English	www2.ncte.org
American Educational Research Association	www.aera.net

Literacy Events and Happenings

International Literacy Association Annual Conference	https://literacyworldwide.org/conference
National Council for Teachers of English Annual Conference	www2.ncte.org/events
Reading Rockets Literacy Calendar	www.readingrockets.org/calendar
ReadWriteThink Calendar Activities	www.readwritethink.org/classroom-resources/calendar-activities/

Figure 2.6: *Resources for current research, professional literature, and events*

learning. Figure 2.7 showcases an infographic I used at the start of a professional development session to generate a conversation about our students' reading lives and the kinds of classroom routines that promote reading.

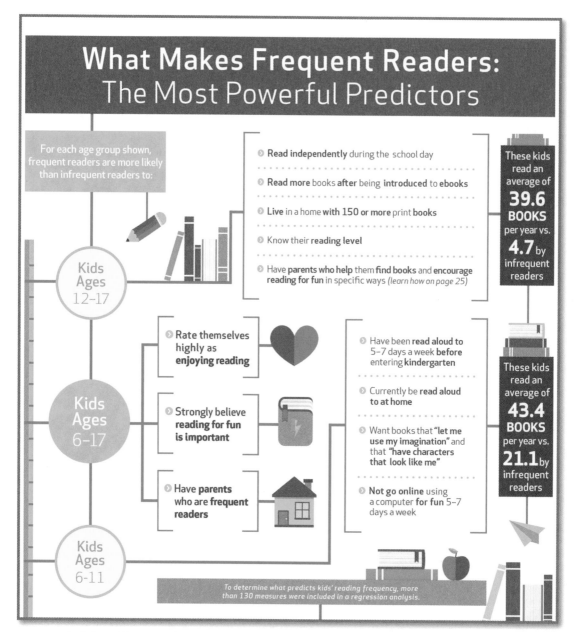

What Makes Frequent Readers: The Most Powerful Predictors

For each age group shown, frequent readers are more likely than infrequent readers to:

Kids Ages 12-17

- Read independently during the school day
- Read more books after being introduced to ebooks
- Live in a home with 150 or more print books
- Know their reading level
- Have parents who help them find books and encourage reading for fun in specific ways (learn how on page 25)

These kids read an average of **39.6 BOOKS** per year vs. **4.7** by infrequent readers

Kids Ages 6-17

- Rate themselves highly as enjoying reading
- Strongly believe reading for fun is important
- Have parents who are frequent readers

- Have been read aloud to 5-7 days a week before entering kindergarten
- Currently be read aloud to at home
- Want books that "let me use my imagination" and that "have characters that look like me"
- Not go online using a computer for fun 5-7 days a week

These kids read an average of **43.4 BOOKS** per year vs. **21.1** by infrequent readers

Kids Ages 6-11

To determine what predicts kids' reading frequency, more than 130 measures were included in a regression analysis.

Figure 2.7: *An infographic summarizing the kids and family reading report from Scholastic*

This graphic sparked a rich conversation about our students' reading lives and helped connect our conversations to actual research and professional literature. Figure 2.8 is an infographic representing the book *Falling in Love with Close Reading* (Lehman and Roberts 2013). I used this to generate interest in the book for an upcoming book club with teachers. Seeing the big picture of the book and the main content presented gave teachers a starting point for their thinking and fueled their desire to read more.

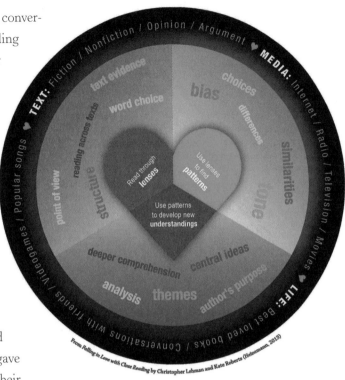

Figure 2.8: *An infographic representing the book* Falling in Love with Close Reading

As infographics gain in popularity, it is easier to find them to support your coaching. Start by visiting the publishers' pages of the books you are interested in to see if there is already one available. Next, visit professional organizations and literacy research institutions, because many often represent summaries of their research in graphic form. You might like to browse my Padlet of infographics as a starting point.

Scan the QR code to view my Padlet of infographics for literacy coaches.
http://bit.ly/2AjEuBg

Can't find the one you need for your own coaching? Then make one! There are multiple infographic tools available to create your own, based on the degree of technical skills needed and the special effects desired. Figure 2.9 offers a list of them to browse.

TOOLS TO CREATE INFOGRAPHICS

Canva Infographic Maker	www.canva.com/create/infographics/
Easelly	www.easel.ly/
Picktochart	https://piktochart.com/
Infogram	https://infogram.com
Venngage	https://venngage.com/

Figure 2.9: *A list of tools to create infographics*

Start by exploring the different tools and browse the infographics others have created to get a sense of the possibilities. Next, think about what you might create an infographic about. A natural starting point might be to share the content of a recently published article with your teachers. Read through the article and note the most pertinent and important content you want to share. Using your chosen infographic tool, add the text and choose complementary graphics. Here are a few tips for creating your own infographic:

1. Choose only the most important information to represent on the infographic.

2. Include related images to support readers' interest and understanding of the topic.

3. Use fonts that are clear and easy to read.

4. Use colors to support your ideas and match your message.

5. Pay attention to size. Larger items will garner the most attention.

Share your newly created infographics with teachers and encourage conversation around them. You might share them in professional development sessions, post them in high-traffic areas for sneaky reading, or include them as part of a book study or inquiry. Encourage teachers to reflect on the information presented, question what information is missing, and spark their curiosity for additional reading and learning. Be sure to have the full-length version of the piece available for later reading, even linking to it with a QR code right on the infographic.

By using infographics in our coaching, not only do we invite inquiry and discussion around research and professional texts, we model how important these kinds of reading, viewing, and critical literacy skills are in our age of literacy, a lesson easily transferred to the classroom.

> **LAUNCHING POINT ✳**
>
> *Want to give infographics a try? Start small and find an infographic that you could use in your next professional development session to spark conversation and inquiry. Find something worth sharing? Tweet it to @AffinitoLit and I will add it to my collection!*

Inspire Unexpected Reading

I love to see children and adults reading at unexpected moments and in unexpected places: in the grocery cart at the supermarket, on the school playground, waiting for the school bus, or even in the doctor's office. It makes me smile to know that child has a strong identity as a reader and knows that reading can happen anywhere we want it to. I remember the time I walked into a pole at the local mall because I just had to start reading the newest Babysitters Club book before I reached the car. Lesson learned? No, I continued that terrible practice each time Ann M. Martin wrote a new book in the series. Readers are compelled to read and make time in their daily schedules to do so. If not naturally, they can be convinced to if the opportunity arises. Consider waiting in line at the grocery store. The shelves are lined with magazines and "smut" magazines, as my great-grandmother would lovingly call them, just waiting to be read, many of us doing just that as we wait. Think about the restrooms in local businesses. Many have advertisements taped to the inner wall of the bathroom stall, understanding that we are indeed a captive audience for their messages. The bottom line (yes, pun intended) is that if the opportunity arises and we are intrigued by what we see, we will read and often welcome the opportunity to do so.

As a literacy coach, you have the power to infuse reading into the culture of a school. How might your teachers respond if they found a personal note from you with a book or an article you knew they would love? Found poems and riddles on the stalls of the bathroom doors? Glanced at interesting blog posts taped to the wall by the microwave?

We all can identify spaces in our school where a bit of reading might inspire or ease situations. Where might you delight in finding a short story? In line for the photocopier? By the door where you do bus duty? Although it may be challenging to tape an interesting research article to the wall to gain teachers' interest, it is quite easy to post a QR code to almost any surface of your school, obviously or inconspicuously. Teachers can then scan the code with any mobile device for quick and easy access to any research article, blog post, video, or instructional resource. Figure 2.10 offers pictures of unexpected places literacy coaches have encouraged reading.

Figure 2.10: *Pictures of text and QR codes placed in unexpected places to spark reading*

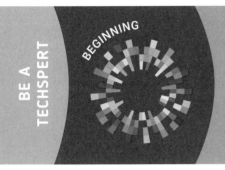

BE A TECHSPERT

BEGINNING

TECH TOOL

QR STUFF: *A QR code generator*
WEBSITE: *www.qrstuff.com*
COST: *Free! Premium plans vary.*
TECHSPERT LEVEL: *Great for beginning tech users*

Wondering what you might attach to the QR codes? You can link to any website, article, or instructional resource, but it can be fun to link to pieces that represent their location as well. Figure 2.11 offers a few ideas to get started.

This kind of unexpected or sneaky reading enhances reading lives, builds camaraderie, and strengthens a community around reading and learning. Teachers can then take this newfound enthusiasm for unexpected reading into their own classrooms, posting QR codes for their students to scan around the classroom. Imagine students' delight when they find a QR code on a window in their classroom and read Wonderopolis' Wonder of the Day on how forecasters predict the weather. Or their surprise when a QR code linked to an article on how to care for a hamster appears on the cage of their beloved class pet. Students can even get in on the fun and share ideas with the teacher on what to post around the room!

LOCATION	TEXT
By the photocopier	The Power of Keeping Your Cool: www.edutopia.org/blog/the-power-keeping-cool-rebecca-alber
In the faculty room	Ten Faces Teachers Make During Staff Meetings: https://boredteachers.com/blogs/the-faculty-room/10-faces-teachers-make-during-staff-meetings
In a school hallway	The Heart of a Teacher Poem: www.simpletruths.com/heart-of-a-teacher-poem.html
By the playground door	NAEYC Article on Recess: http://oldweb.naeyc.org/community/uploads/Stupianskyrecessarticle.pdf

Figure 2.11: *Ideas for unexpected reading*

I just know your mind is spinning with ideas, so go ahead and give one a try! Identify a location of your school that would benefit from some unexpected reading and choose a text to link to. Follow these three easy steps to connect your text to a QR code.

1. *Copy the Internet address of the text you would like to link to.*
2. *Visit www.qrstuff.com and paste the link into the QR code generator. Click "Download QR Code."*
3. *Copy the QR code and paste it onto the LOOK template provided in the online resources for this book or create your own. Add the title of the online resource to pique teachers' curiosity. Save your QR code for later reference, if you choose.*

Now, the fun begins! Place your QR somewhere in your school for teachers to enjoy and let the reading begin! Snap a picture of it and tweet it to @AffinitoLit to share with other readers!

One kindergarten teacher decided to infuse her room with QR codes to inspire students to read, watch, and learn. See Figure 2.12 to see how she linked QR codes to early leveled readers from www.uniteforliteracy.com and engaging videos from www.thekidshouldseethis.com and posted them around the room. Students use the class iPads to scan the codes during free time to sneak in extra learning.

Figure 2.12: *Pictures of a kindergarten classroom that uses QR codes to link students to engaging books and media*

Create Spaces for Learning

Where do you work best? Do you prefer to work at your desk at school? Do you prefer your home office tucked away in a corner of your house? Regardless of where you prefer to work, the space you create for your work as literacy coach is personalized to the work you do and the things you need to do it with. You might have your desk with your needed laptop and sticky notes. You might have a bookshelf with your most treasured professional books. Or, if you are like me, you have multiple bags: a bag for schools, a bag for the university, and a bag for my own reading and writing, all stored not so neatly in the trunk of my car for easy access wherever I need them.

The spaces we create to host our work as literacy leaders and coaches matter. They are rooms that invite and inspire. They often house shelves of children's books, professional texts for teachers, beautiful displays of teacher and student practice, and all the tools needed for teacher learning and collaboration. Allison and Maria, literacy coaches in upstate New York, have carefully designed their rooms to support teacher collaboration and inquiry into instructional practices. See Figures 2.13 through 2.18 for pictures of Allison and Maria's literacy coaching spaces.

Figure 2.13 (above): *Anchor charts on determining theme*

Figure 2.14 (left): *Examples of teaching tools*

Figure 2.15: *A well-stocked, leveled lending library*

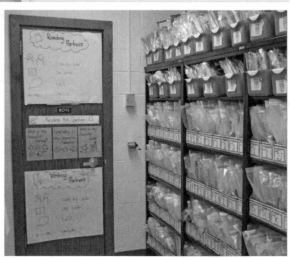

Figure 2.16: *A comfortable meeting space*

Figure 2.17: *Available coaching materials and resources*

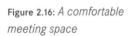

Figure 2.18: *Model anchor charts posted on the door*

Although our own coaching spaces are unique to our positions and schools, there are a few common elements that support teacher collaboration and learning:

1. **The rooms are inviting:** The spaces we create for teachers need to invite them in. This space needs to be a refuge from the stresses and challenges of teaching and should renew teachers' energy and enthusiasm for teaching.

2. **The rooms act as models for student learning:** Literacy coaches model possibilities for student learning. Arrange the layout of your room and wall space to mirror that of an effective classroom and inspire teachers to do the same.

3. **There are libraries of books and professional resources:** Stock your coaching space with books, books, and more books. Model what an effective classroom library and reading corner might look like. Share your top book choices and have book recommendations readily available for teachers.

4. **They are stocked with tools of collaboration:** Coaching spaces need plenty of materials for teacher collaboration: large chart paper, sticky notes, pens, pencils, highlighters, laptops or other devices, and plenty of chocolate in colorful bowls.

5. **There is a comfortable meeting area:** Although classrooms might be excellent models for teaching, kid-sized tables and chairs are not conducive to teacher learning. Ensure that you have the space needed to comfortably seat a group of teachers around a table for discussion and collaborative work.

Our coaching spaces should encourage and celebrate learning. Imagine if we had collaborative spaces where at each visit teachers had something new to ponder? A newly published children's literature text? A display of new professional resources available to teachers? A Wonder Wall where teachers posted their ideas and questions, just as we might do for students? A bulletin board showcasing QR codes that link to thought-provoking articles, blogs, and other pieces of reading? When we create places for teachers to wonder, to inquire, and to take instructional risks with the support of others, we transform the atmosphere of the school. Digital tools can help cultivate and support teacher collaboration in in-person, digital, online, and virtual ways to inspire teacher learning.

Host Digital Book Clubs

Learning is social. When we discuss new ideas together, they multiply. Our collective experiences and ideas and our shared learning make us stronger together than we are apart. I am sure many of you reading this book have participated in some type of book club: a personal book club with friends, a voluntary book club with colleagues around a shared text, or even a mandated professional text by your district. It can be challenging to find the time for these kinds of experiences, but digital tools can enhance and even replace face-to-face meetings.

Participation in the #cyberPD virtual book talk was a transforming experience for my career. The Google+ Community for #cyberPD describes the project as "an event to connect educators in collaborative professional conversation. Through blogs, Twitter, and the digital media, participants share thinking around a common professional title featured for discussion. Though the main event is in July of each year, the conversations and connections carry across the year" (2016). This was my first experience in an online book study, outside of my academic experiences, where teachers across the world voluntarily and freely connected to discuss a common text. The camaraderie was instant as we dove into the text, blogging, tweeting and posting on the Google+ Community. Fortunately for us, the authors of the text joined in the event and participated throughout the summer. I met new colleagues, many of whom I continue to work with today, and I was energized by the work of the group. I learned some very important lessons that continue to guide my work:

1. Engaging in digital book study expands what is possible. We used print, audio, and video discussions that were both synchronous and asynchronous. Teachers chose the level and type of participation that worked best for them.

2. Learning is never complete and the goal is to improve instruction for our students. I continued my own learning and gained new teaching skills and strategies. Sharing our work with others inspired us to try more, do more, and be more for the sake of our students.

3. We all have ideas worth sharing. I received comments that validated my work and congratulated my efforts. The experience showed me that even if we have doubts, the community will support you.

The #cyberPD group is only one example of the many different opportunities available to engage in inquiry with others. See Figure 2.19 for additional online book studies you might be interested in.

ONLINE BOOK STUDIES

#cyberPD	https://plus.google.com/u/0/communities/107711243109928665922
Heinemann Professional Development: Teaching and Learning Community	www.facebook.com/groups/summerplc
The Reading and Writing Strategies Book Community	www.facebook.com/groups/ReadingStrategiesBook/
Literacy Teacher Book Club	www.facebook.com/groups/1738331936446879/
Fountas & Pinnell Literacy Community	www.facebook.com/groups/FountasPinnell/

Figure 2.19: *A list of literacy online book studies*

Typically, book studies are done in person, after school, and with colleagues we see on a daily basis. Although we will learn from one another, real learning happens when we listen to new voices and gain different perspectives and ideas. By enhancing your current book study with online, digital tools, you can widen the conversation and energize the thinking of all. Or you might choose to participate completely online and discuss the text virtually. Follow the lead of your teachers and choose what works best for them, slowly introducing new ideas from outside your school walls. Here are a few possibilities:

1. Enhance your in-person book club with digital resources. Print and share a blog post or other online resource about your chosen text. Encourage teachers to reflect on this new content and how a different, outside perspective enriches the conversation and the learning.

2. Incorporate social media into your book club sessions. Pull up the Twitter hashtag dedicated to the book and scroll through the comments to spark conversations at the start of your session. If there is a Facebook group dedicated to the book, share pertinent posts and resources from it with your teachers.

3. Create a digital space for discussions between meeting sessions. Create a private Google+ Community, Facebook group or even a Padlet wall for your teachers to

share their reflections in between meetings, which can inform how you plan for your in-person meeting time.

4. Finally, you might take your learning public. Encourage your teachers to share their individual or group reflections with the wider audience. Participate in public book studies together and let your teachers feel the professional power that comes from knowing you are impacting the learning of other teachers.

Broadening our perspective helps us consider new ideas that benefit our students. Once teachers see the power in connecting with others for the sake of professional learning, they might provide the same opportunities for their students, connecting with other classrooms around the world or even with authors themselves. Teachers can partner with other classrooms reading the same book and lead class book discussions through Google Hangout or Skype. Students can share responses and questions about the books they are reading by using Google+ Communities or Google Classroom. They can also read what other students are saying. By connecting students with other classrooms, they hear different perspectives and realize just how expansive and accessible the world outside the classroom is.

LAUNCHING POINT
✳

Identify a book you are currently reading or plan to read with teachers. Search the title of the book in social media sites, such as Twitter or Facebook. Scroll through the posts and save compelling tweets and links to share with your teachers. You might start a file to save them for easy reference later on in your sessions and in your coaching.

CONNECTION TO THE CLASSROOM
✳

After meeting in book clubs, Mary's fourth-grade students shared their thinking with the class on a shared Padlet. During share time, the teacher pulls the Padlet up on the SMART Board. See Figure 2.20 for an example.

Her students now regularly share their thinking on Padlet in multiple ways: their own Padlet reading walls, shared book club thinking, and even questions of the week based on a particular skill, such as characterization. These digital bulletin boards link students together digitally and strengthen learning through collaboration with others.

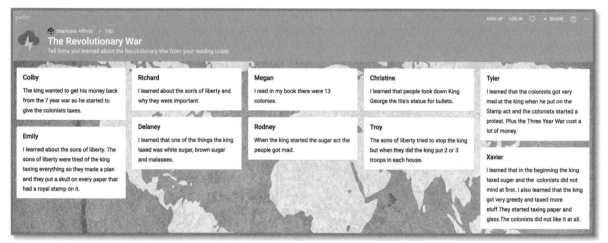

Figure 2.20: *A screenshot of a Padlet wall used in a reading workshop share session*

Leverage Digital Communities

There is great power in participating in a digital community. Many online learning communities are designed to support teacher learning. Figure 2.21 provides a list of powerful learning communities you might be interested in joining.

Find one that meets your interests and goals. Feel the power in these groups and then create your own community page for the teachers you work with. These shared digital communities provide new outlets for conversation, strengthen community building, and showcase teaching and learning efforts, often hatching new instructional ideas in the process. By removing participation barriers and the walls that divide us, we reimagine our teaching and learning in new, digital spaces and open new possibilities for learning and collaborating with others.

Creating a Google+ Community for your teachers is an ideal place to start. Google+ Communities are groups or forums built to bring people together around particular topics. These pages can be created and organized in a variety of ways for teachers to have safe spaces for collaboration and inquiry.

DIGITAL COMMUNITIES

Heinemann Professional Learning Facebook Page

Picture Book 10 for 10 Google+ Community

The Reading Strategies Book Facebook Community Page

Amplify Facebook Community Group

Units of Study Facebook Pages

International Society for Technology in Education (ISTE) Teacher Education Network Google+ Community

ISTE Ed Tech Coaches PLN Google+ Community

International Literacy Association Google+ Community

Figure 2.21: *A list of digital communities for literacy coaches*

Shelly Fenton, a literacy coach in upstate New York, created a Google+ Community page focused on reading workshop, a new initiative in her district. Membership in the group was voluntary; it was a place where teachers could share ideas, ask questions, and celebrate practice as they shifted how they taught literacy in the classroom. Over time, she has revised the space to include categories for posts and easy access to important resources, supporting collaboration within and across her various elementary buildings. Figure 2.22 showcases the opening page of her Google+ Community.

Here are some of the "must includes" for your digital learning community:

✳ a description of the community and the purpose for creating it

✳ links to important documents and sites relevant to your work together

✳ posting categories for easy posting and searching.

It is important to post regularly to encourage conversation and collaboration. Model the kinds of interactions you hope your teachers will have in the group. Figures 2.23 to 2.25 show screenshots of Shelley's posts to encourage connections and collaboration among teachers. In these posts, Shelley:

✳ shares research and resources

✳ showcases classroom efforts

✳ documents coaching and classroom events

✳ poses questions and invites inquiry.

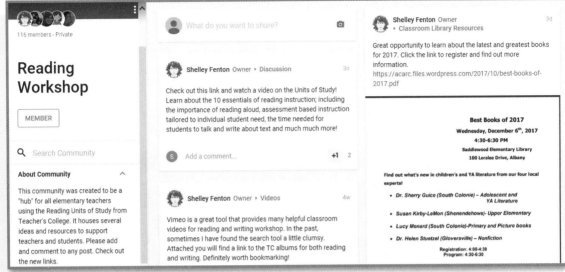

Figure 2.22 (above): *The opening page of Shelley Fenton's Reading Workshop Google+ Community*

Figure 2.23 (top left): *Shelley's post to showcase and celebrate student learning*

Figure 2.24 (bottom left): *Shelley's post to share resources she created for teachers*

Figure 2.25 (below): *Shelley's post to celebrate student learning with a teacher's response*

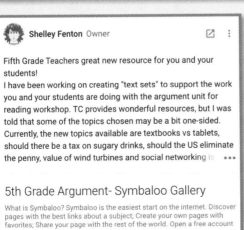

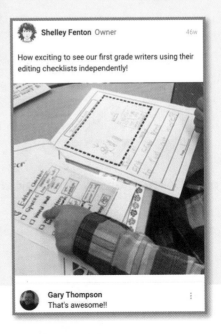

If your school does not use Google, you might create a private Facebook group for your teachers. Like Google+ Communities, you can create a community to share news and updates, interesting blog posts and articles, and daily tidbits of inspiration with teachers. Teachers can also post their own ideas to the page, starting digital conversations to inspire further collaboration.

BE A TECHSPERT

BEGINNING

TECH TOOL

FACEBOOK: *Online social networking site*
WEBSITE: *http://facebook.com*
COST: *Free!*
TECHSPERT LEVEL: *Great for beginning tech users*

Regardless of the method you choose, creating a digital space to connect and collaborate with teachers will break down the boundaries between classroom doors and strengthen communication within your school.

LAUNCHING POINT ✳

Create a Google+ digital community space for the teachers you work with. After entering the Communities tab in your Google+ profile, click on "Yours" and then create a new community. You will be prompted to name the community and choose your privacy settings. Personalize your page by adding in a description of your group and creating categories for posting. Invite your teachers to your newly created page and start with a welcoming post that describes the page and your purpose for it. Share an interesting article and link to a resource teachers might enjoy. Return often and watch your community thrive!

Forge Connections with Innovative Tools

Digital apps can intensify our collaborative efforts and forge pathways previously not possible. Voxer is a mobile messaging app that combines text, voice, photo, and video messages for powerful collaboration.

BE A TECHSPERT

INTERMEDIATE

TECH TOOL

VOXER: *A mobile messaging app*
WEBSITE: *http://voxer.com*
COST: *Free! Premium plans vary.*
TECHSPERT LEVEL: *Good for intermediate tech users*

I was first introduced to Voxer through participation in the #cyberPD group. A small group of us were interested in continuing our conversations together after our scheduled book study was complete. We connected through Voxer and discussed how we were transferring our learning to the classroom. As you can see from Figure 2.26 we utilized a combination of text and audio messages to share new ideas and collaborate.

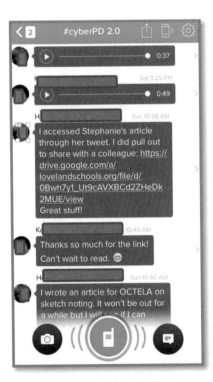
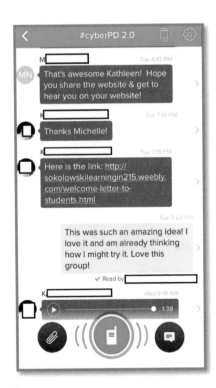

Figure 2.26: *A screenshot of a #cyberPD Voxer conversation*

So how might you use this in your work with teachers?

* Create a Voxer group for your school faculty as a communication tool. Send out morning messages, inspirational stories, or new book titles to share in the classroom.

* Create a smaller Voxer group for teachers interested in similar topics for inquiry and conversation.

* Create a digital book study through Voxer.

* Connect with individual teachers through Voxer as a coaching tool. Use it to make coaching plans, debrief after lessons, and stay connected throughout the year.

When we think differently about how we define collaboration and the spaces we engage in such work, we reimagine teaching and learning and see new possibilities for our work together, often widening our professional learning networks (PLNs) in the process as we encounter new ideas and meet new educators.

> **LAUNCHING POINT ✳**
>
> *Before you use Voxer in your coaching with teachers, you need to try it for yourself. First, download the Voxer app and create a profile. Next, scan the following QR code for an extensive listing of Voxer groups for educators created by Heather Gauck, Karen Corbell, and Sarah Thomas. Choose one that interests you and follow the directions to join. Introduce yourself and join the conversation!*
>
>
> Scan the QR code for an extensive listing of Voxer groups.
> http://bit.ly/12I8iCu

Expand Professional Learning Networks

Collaboration begins with connections. As a literacy coach, you have opportunities to work with a number of teachers across multiple personalities, grade levels, and interests. Helping teachers seek out connections with others fuels their creativity and generates a feeling of support, of a connected community. Sometimes, we are lucky enough to find these connections within our own schools, but sometimes we need or want to search elsewhere to forge those professional bonds, expanding our PLNs.

Crowley (2014) defines a PLN as a vibrant ever-changing group of connections where teachers both share and learn, reflecting our values, passions, and areas of expertise. I have found quite helpful Crowley's analogy of likening a PLN to the rippled waters that are layered when tossing a rock into the water. The smallest inner ring represents the teachers we work with, our friends, and our close mentors, and is typically cultivated in person. These are the people we see and interact with daily. They understand our teaching contexts, work alongside us, and provide the needed, day-to-day support and camaraderie that only close colleagues provide. The middle ring represents those we connect with who have the same passions and interests as we do. These connections might be found in our own schools, but often are those we meet and connect with because of our professional interests. These might be teachers we met at a professional development session or educators who are part of a book club we participate in. This middle layer of teachers fuels our passions and motivates our continued work. The outer layer comprises the literacy professionals and researchers we look up to and learn from. Although they are physically the farthest away from our classrooms, with the help of technology and digital tools we can easily connect and learn from those leading our field. Here's how.

Harness the Power of Social Media

Technology and social media have transformed the ways we connect with others. No longer are we limited by time and location. At the touch of a keyboard we have access to communities of learners that connect us, provide access to new resources, and widen our personal learning networks. Social media offers particular opportunities to forge professional connections with others.

Many of our students, even the younger ones, are well versed in the workings of social media. Students post, tag, like, comment, reply, and share snippets of their lives and interests on Instagram, Facebook, Snapchat, and more. They use these tools to stay connected to their friends, entertain themselves based on their interests, and learn new facts and information. Yet, although this kind of activity comes naturally, do they use those very same tools for reading, writing, and learning? Probably not, and I would argue the same could be said for teachers. Although many of your teachers use social media in their personal lives, sharing pictures and updates with family and friends, they might not realize the untapped potential it holds for their professional lives as well.

Twitter offers particular promise for forging professional connections. Twitter is an online social networking and microblogging platform where users send and read short posts, or tweets, up to 280 characters. Using Twitter, we can:

* share resources with other educators

* participate in real-time professional development chats

* communicate with teachers and school faculty

* keep up-to-date on research and professional literature

* receive updates from professional literacy organizations

* connect with other professionals on common goals.

BE A TECHSPERT

INTERMEDIATE

TECH TOOL

TWITTER: *Online social networking site*
WEBSITE: *http://twitter.com*
COST: *Free!*
TECHSPERT LEVEL: *Good for intermediate tech users*

If Twitter is new to you, scan the QR code for a free, informative webinar from Heinemann called "Twitter for Educators." It provides an engaging overview using Twitter in education and offers concrete steps for getting started.

Scan the QR code to view Heinemann's "Twitter for Educators" webinar.
http://bit.ly/1KSe3zF

If you do not have one already, create a professional profile that represents the work you do. Although some teachers use their personal accounts professionally, I recommend that you create a separate account for your work as a literacy coach to maintain personal privacy.

Next, follow literacy mentors and professionals who can inspire your work with their micro-writing and resources. Start by following the authors and researchers you most admire and watch your feed grow. Next, send out tweets to the authors of your book study books and let them know you are engaging with their work. Retweet and like their contributions and connect with their like-minded followers too. Figure 2.27 offers a sampling of the literacy mentors and colleagues I follow on Twitter.

Cultivate your own Twitter account and post updates, links to engaging articles, resources to share, and simple messages of inspiration to your teachers. These might be general posts for all or you might tag specific teachers to connect them to materials and ideas you think might be a good fit for them.

Twitter chats provide free professional learning and collaboration with others through social media. Participants tweet at particular times on particular topics using hashtags to link their conversations.

LITERACY PROFESSIONAL	TWITTER HANDLE
John Schu	@MrSchuReads
Pernille Ripp	@pernilleripp
Sara K. Ahmed	@SaraKAhmed
Kristen Ziemke	@KristenZiemke
Donalyn Miller	@donalynbooks
Franki Sibberson	@frankisibberson
Kwame Alexander	@kwamealexander
Chris Lehman	@iChrisLehman
Mary Howard	@DrMaryHoward
Carol Jago	@CarolJago
Wendy Kopp	@WendyKopp
Cornelius Minor	@MisterMinor

Figure 2.27: *Literacy professionals to follow on Twitter*

LAUNCHING POINT

Stop reading and head to Twitter. Choose a colleague or two from the list above and search for his or her Twitter handle. Scroll through the Twitter feed and simply see what you can learn. You might find new nuggets of inspiration, links to helpful instructional resources, announcements of upcoming conferences and workshops, and tweets that get you thinking. Give yourself permission to enjoy a few minutes reading the microwriting of others and see what you can learn.

NCTE hosts #NCTEchat on the third Sunday of each month at 8 p.m. Eastern time. The #G2Great chat meets each Thursday night at 8:30 p.m. Eastern time and features a variety of literacy professionals, authors, and topics each week. Each chat is dedicated to a specialized topic with facilitators chosen based on their expertise and interests. Together, participants learn from the collective intelligence of the group, gaining new perspectives and ideas, classroom lessons and resources, tools and teaching ideas, and innovative insights. Chats are typically archived for later viewing and reflection, often just as useful as the live event. The site www.participate.com /chats curates all known Twitter chats through a collaborative calendar. You can easily search the calendar for chats you might be interested in. These "fast chats" pack a flurry of tweets and intellectual activity into a short amount of time. However, "slow chats" offer the same kind of thinking and learning, but stretched out over a longer period, making it easier to enter into the conversation. You might start with a slow chat mentality and simply browse the Twitter feeds of the chats and lurk around the archive to learn more. However, there is simply nothing like participating in a live chat event. The fast-paced conversation, the high energy of participations, and the flurry of professional microwriting is simply amazing. You meet new colleagues, connect with others, gain professional advice and wisdom, and leave with a new perspective and instructional resources to try tomorrow. But give yourself room to explore and grow. In my first live chat, I was overwhelmed, fell behind on answering questions, and was ready to give up. I couldn't read the posts, respond to them, like them, add a new "tweep" to follow, and process the new information I was getting simultaneously. I felt like a Twitter failure. But I didn't give up. Instead, I started with slow chats and attempted fast chats, but did not worry if I could not keep all or participate the entire time (especially because my kids are very good interrupters!). I was sure to check the archive or browse the feed the next day. Over time, I became more proficient at chatting and continue to be amazed at how empowered and energized I feel every time a chat ends. The professional power and connectedness I feel is unmatched. I highly recommend setting the time aside to participate in a Twitter chat in some way. Don't worry if you are slow to start and feel like you will never catch up. You will and will be even better the next time around. Trust me.

BLOGS TO FOLLOW

Perspectives	www.teachersforteachers.net
A Year of Reading	http://readingyear.blogspot.com
Burkins & Yaris	www.burkinsandyaris.com/whos-doing-the-work-blog/
Literacy Lenses	www.literacylenses.com/
indent	www.kateandmaggie.com/blog/
Nerdy Book Club	https://nerdybookclub.wordpress.com
Two Writing Teachers	https://twowritingteachers.org
chartchums	https://chartchums.wordpress.com
Reflect & Refine	http://reflectandrefine.blogspot.com

Figure 2.28: *My favorite blogs to follow*

In our exploration of social media, we often find powerful blog posts that capture the teaching and learning journeys of others. Figure 2.28 gives a listing of my favorite blogs.

When you find a blog that speaks to you, say so. Comment on the posts that resonate and start following bloggers on their social media accounts to stay connected and receive updates. You might even use a blogging service, such as Bloglovin', to compile your favorite blogs in one place.

BE A TECHSPERT

BEGINNING

TECH TOOL

BLOGLOVIN': *Curates multiple blogs into one feed*
WEBSITE: *www.bloglovin.com*
COST: *Free!*
TECHSPERT LEVEL: *Great for beginning tech users*

One of the most treasured parts of my day is enjoying my morning cup of coffee (or two) in the early hours of the day, scrolling through my blog feed, while my family is still sleeping. I feel connected, energized, and ready for the day ahead, comforted by the fact that I am surrounding myself with like-minded inspiration.

Connect with Mentors Digitally and Virtually

Technology affords us access to colleagues, materials, and resources previously not possible. We have access to top-notch literacy professionals, researchers, and children's authors at the click of a button. I have a fairly reluctant reader at home and work to convey the role that books and reading for pleasure could play in his life. We recently had a breakthrough moment and for the first time, he chose to read for a longer period than required. After reading, he suggested I email Lauren Tarshis to tell her just what an important moment this was for us. I sent her a quick tweet instead and within a day, my son had a response (see Figure 2.29).

Figure 2.29: *My Twitter exchange with Lauren Tarshis*

He was amazed at her response and personal message. I was amazed at just how quickly we connected with the author. In my own childhood, I would write letters to my favorite authors and if I received a response, it was typically a generic letter received weeks or even months later. Now, my own children experience instant connections with authors, igniting their enthusiasm as readers and opening new possibilities for their reading lives.

Technology can ignite teacher enthusiasm for literacy learning, just as it did for my own son. We can chat with our favorite literacy professionals on Twitter, share ideas through Facebook community groups, and interact through Google Hangouts and webinars. In my first year of #cyberPD, a virtual book study group, we studied *Digital Reading* by Bill Bass and Frankie Sibberson (2015). The authors participated in the event and even replied to my blog posts and tweets throughout the summer, amplifying my enthusiasm and learning. Technology fueled these connections and had an immediate and long-lasting impact on my own learning, coaching, and vision for my work ahead.

Webinars, or Web-based seminars, are streamed webcasts that include presentation materials and resources, live discussions with presenters and even other participants, video demonstrations, and links to continued discussions on social media. As a coach, you might first utilize these webinars to further your own professional learning. Learn new ideas, engage in shared learning experiences with other coaches and teachers, and transfer your learning to your own coaching. I provide a list of my go-to sites in Figure 2.30.

WEBINARS AND WEBCASTS	ARCHIVED RECORDING ADDRESS
Heinemann Online PD	www.heinemann.com/PD/online/default.aspx
The Educator Collaborative	https://theeducatorcollaborative.com
Association for Supervision and Curriculum Development	www.ascd.org/professional-development/webinars.aspx
Reading Rockets	www.readingrockets.org/webcasts
Education Week	www.edweek.org/ew/marketplace/webinars/webinars.html

Figure 2.30: *A list of useful webinars and webcasts for literacy coaches*

You might also use these webinars in your sessions with teachers, igniting your professional development sessions with virtual interactions with nationally recognized literacy professionals. Although webinars are ideally viewed live to enable synchronous communication with the presenter and other participants, these webinars are typically recorded and archived for later use as well. Use portions of them in your professional development sessions to enhance your in-person learning experiences. Play a clip of a literacy researcher sharing a summary of research to inspire conversation. Share a section of a webinar that showcased a new idea for literacy instruction. You might even share the transcript or Twitter archive of a particular webinar and encourage comments and reflection. Regardless of how you choose to use the webinars, they can add a new element of interaction and inspiration to your work.

Many researchers and authors also offer professional development and consulting through Google Hangout, Skype, or other platforms such as Zoom. Imagine what would happen if you could interact with the author of your book study? Or pose questions to the researcher whose work guides your intervention program? Virtual meeting tools erase the geographical boundaries that separate us and provide access to learning that might previously be unattainable. The Albany City Area Reading Council provides a range of events and gatherings for literacy teachers in New York. One of the most innovative was an after-school Skype session with Kristin Ziemke. Teachers met after school in Albany and connected with Kristin through Skype. She shared a presentation and engaged with the audience as if she were right in the room. Not only was this a powerful experience in exploring digital literacy, it was a powerful experience for teacher learning as well. Teachers buzzed not only about the new information they were learning, but about the innovative way they learned it. Traditional professional development was abandoned and technology was used to make connections.

Whether you participate in person or online, synchronously or asynchronously, technology provides new possibilities for shared teacher learning. By connecting with prominent figures in our field and lessening the distance between them, teachers develop powerful inspiration for the classroom that may not have previously existed. This kind of learning is contagious. If teachers feel empowered and motivated to connect with their most treasured literacy professionals, then their students might feel empowered and motivated to connect with the authors important to them as well. By broadening the connections our teachers make, they can begin to broaden the connections their students can make in the classroom, opening a new world of learning for all.

LAUNCHING POINT ✳

Let's make a connection for our students right now. Scan the following QR code to visit Kate Messner's "Authors Who Skype with Classes & Book Clubs (For Free!)" webpage and browse the authors you might interact with in your school. Choose one and reach out to the author to learn about the possibilities available for your teachers and students.

Scan the QR code to see a list of authors who Skype.
http://bit.ly/1uFscGf

Participate in Global Literacy Events

The International Literacy Association recently changed its name from the International Reading Association to the Interactional Literacy Association to reflect a more encompassing view of literacy and literacy instruction. The bold mission statement on the home page is clear: "The ability to READ, WRITE, and COMMUNICATE connects people and empowers them to achieve things they never thought possible. It truly is the basis of who we are and how we interact with the world" (ILA 2016). It is a powerful statement. Literacy isn't only about learning how to read the words on the page; it is about reading the world and leaving our mark on it. Technology and digital tools provide access and connection previously not possible. Together, we read and write for reasons larger than ourselves: to connect, to learn from one another, and to enact positive change. To that end, there are multiple virtual events, projects, and movements that we can participate in to learn from others and become part of something bigger than ourselves and our own classrooms. Some of these events are exclusively for teachers and others invite student participation as well, showing our students just how powerful reading and writing can be.

IT'S MONDAY, WHAT ARE YOU READING?

Consider starting a new reading tradition in your school called "It's Monday, What Are You Reading?" (IMWAYR), an idea I first encountered from @TeachMentorTexts and @UnleashingReaders. The premise is simple: Each Monday, readers share the texts they are reading with other readers. Here are a few ways to get involved:

※ Make a habit of asking teachers and students about the books they are reading each Monday.

※ Dedicate a whiteboard or glitter board in your coaching space to writing the titles your teachers are reading each week.

※ Create an IMWAYR Padlet wall for your school. Encourage teachers to post about the books they are reading in their classrooms.

※ Create video book talks to share with the school. Create a recording station in your coaching space with an iPad or laptop, microphone, and a curtain. Each Monday, record a children's book introduction/recommendation to share with the school. Share your recommendations on the Monday morning announcements, email the weekly recommendations to teachers each Monday, or even house them on a Padlet wall that you create.

※ Move it to the classroom. Invite teachers to connect to your IMWAYR initiative. Start small and have students write their Monday book titles on sticky notes to post on their classroom door. Or, create digital Padlet walls for each classroom and encourage teachers to have their students share their own reading as well.

※ Take your reading public and share your titles with the world using the #IMWAYR hashtag.

LAUNCHING POINT ※

Let's pretend it is Monday. So, it's Monday, what are you reading? Tweet your titles to @AffinitoLit and #IMWAYR. Browse the feed and add a few titles to your To-Be-Read (TBR) stack!

#BOOKADAY AND #CLASSROOMBOOKADAY

The #bookaday and #classroombookaday hashtags are other exciting reading initiatives. Created by Donalyn Miller and Jillian Heise, these initiatives are true to their names: teachers read aloud a text to their students each day and celebrate the book by keeping a visual display of the books read throughout the school year. As a literacy coach, you might:

1. Follow the #bookaday and #classroombookaday hashtags to learn about new children's literature titles to share with your teachers. Get inspired by the many books classrooms are reading!

2. Vow to read at least one book in a classroom each day as a coach and post to the hashtag.

3. Share the #classroombookaday concept with teachers and encourage them to try it in their classrooms with your support. Showcase the read-alouds on a Padlet wall to share with parents.

4. Team up with the school librarian and create a #bookaday display for teachers to easily find and borrow a new read-aloud.

THE GLOBAL READ ALOUD

The Global Read Aloud is an event designed to elicit reading, conversation, and writing with other teachers and students around the world. Over the course of six weeks, teachers read a chosen book aloud to their students with the intent to read, discuss, and make as many global connections as possible. In 2015, over 200,000 teachers and their students participated in the project, including myself. My graduate students and I read *The Year of Billy Miller* (Henkes 2013) and discussed it as a class. We participated in Twitter chats, joined the Facebook group, and even interacted with a class in Malaysia through Padlet. Because I did not have my own elementary classroom at the time, I lived vicariously through those that did, following the #GRABillyMiller hashtag and sharing my experiences with my teacher colleagues. We were in awe at the sheer amount of learning by both teachers and students. Teachers were learning new ways to interact with students, trying new technology tools, and reimagining what it meant to be a reader in the twenty-first century. Students were listening to amazing texts, connecting with students across the country and across the world, even engaging with the author of the book through Twitter, blogging, Google Hangouts, and Skype. The message was powerful: reading can connect the world, and together we can do great things. That inspiring message fueled our work and helped us think differently about literacy instruction for the rest of the school year.

There are other events that are not bound by the calendar or the classroom that could inspire your teachers and students. See Figure 2.31 for a listing of virtual literacy events you might participate in with your teachers, and even their students.

VIRTUAL LITERACY EVENTS

The Global Read Aloud	https://theglobalreadaloud.com
World Read Aloud Day	www.litworld.org/wrad/
International Literacy Day	www.literacyworldwide.org/about-us/news-events/international-literacy-day
NEA's Read Across America	www.nea.org/grants/886.htm
International Dot Day	www.thedotclub.org/dotday/
Scholastic's Celebrate National Poetry Month	http://teacher.scholastic.com/poetry/
Get Caught Reading	www.getcaughtreading.org
National Day on Writing	www.ncte.org/dayonwriting
World Storytelling Day	www.worldstorytellingday.org/
Children's Book Week	www.childrensbookweek.org

Figure 2.31: *A list of virtual literacy events*

LAUNCHING POINT ✳

Visit one of the virtual literacy events posted. Find one that might appeal to your teachers and teachers. Commit to learn more and imagine the possibilities. Share your ideas with your administrator and see what happens next!

Let teachers and students become something bigger than themselves and their classrooms. The rippling effect of stretching ourselves as learners and as educators has a powerful impact on literacy teaching in the classroom. Reach out to others, broaden your horizons, and envision new possibilities by connecting with colleagues and reenergizing your literacy coaching and teaching.

Choose Intentional Coaching Goals

Armed with the information from this chapter, where might you begin? Use the "If-Then-With" chart in Figure 2.32 to help choose an international coaching goal for your work ahead. It will easily pair you with a pedagogical focus and a small group of select tools to help you get started.

IF YOU WANT TO . . .	THEN . . .	WITH THESE TOOLS . . .
Cultivate reading and learning in your school	Connect with teachers around our reading lives	Goodreads, Bookopolis, Padlet, QR codes
	Spark interest in professional reading	Infogram, Picktochart, Canva
	Inspire unexpected reading	QR codes
Create spaces for learning	Host digital book clubs	Google+ Communities, Facebook
	Create digital communities	Google+ Communities, Facebook
	Try innovative tools to connect teachers	Voxer
Expand professional learning networks	Harness social media	Twitter, Facebook, Instagram, Pinterest
	Connect with mentors digitally and virtually	Webinars and webcasts, Google Hangout, Skype, Twitter
	Participate in global literacy events	Twitter, Padlet, Facebook

Figure 2.32: *Use the "If-Then-With" chart to choose intentional literacy coaching goals.*

CHAPTER 2

Redesign
Professional Development

CHAPTER
3

I recently learned to how to downhill ski to keep up with my more adventurous family. How could I possibly let my three children travel thousands of feet up in the air and then travel down twisty paths and slippery slopes alone? I couldn't. So, my husband and I decided to learn to ski. We started off with a group lesson to help get us started. We learned how to slide, snowplow, and stop. We started small, sidestepping our way up the bunny hill a few feet and sliding down. We listened to our instructor, and ourselves, as we attempted each maneuver. We used the feedback from our coach, and our bodies, to better our positions and stay on our feet longer. Off the mountain, we watched videos of successful skiers, learned about helpful drills that would help us turn and stop more readily, and gained motivation to continue. Over time and practice, eventually we wound up at the top of the summit and made it to the bottom successfully. As I continued to ski throughout the season, I was struck by how difficult it was to ski after taking a few days off. When we skied for multiple days in a row, I could clearly see the difference the regular practice had on our abilities. This same kind of thinking applies to learning in general. To get better at something, we must engage in it often and develop a mind-set for improving our skills and our efficacy. Learning is continual and as literacy coaches we must cultivate the kind of culture in our schools that celebrates teachers and students as lifelong learners. Pam Allyn (2015) has said that "reading is like breathing in and writing is like breathing out." Lifelong learning should feel like inhaling and exhaling, a natural part of what we do as educators.

The very idea of literacy coaching acknowledges the faulty assumptions about teacher learning that guided our professional development efforts in the past and emerges from a social constructivist approach. Rather than train teachers through transferring predetermined pedagogical content knowledge, literacy coaches work alongside teachers, coconstructing knowledge. As literacy coaches, we do not position ourselves as experts, but as fellow readers, writers, thinkers, and learners. When we engage *with* teachers, rather than *at* teachers, we send teachers a clear message we are in this journey of teaching and learning together, as fellow colleagues with a common goal, not as experts with an agenda to fix what is wrong with their teaching. Together, teachers and coaches become learners for the sake of the students.

Why It's Important to Redesign Professional Development

Teachers have the power to shape the future. We are educating our future doctors, lawyers, businesspeople, and service workers. The future president of the United States could be sitting in your school at this very moment. What we do each day impacts the kinds of human beings our students will become—the ways we set up our classroom community, the instructional practices we engage in, and the ways we talk to students. For teachers to inspire student learning and make the kind of impact that lasts a lifetime, they must be supported through authentic, relevant, and meaningful learning experiences so they can do what they do best: inspire learning in their own classrooms.

If we do not attend to our own needs as learners, then we cannot possibly take care of the instructional needs of our students. We must continue to learn ourselves and participate in thriving learning communities that fuel our minds and our work. Figure 3.1 lists organizations and communities designed to support our professional learning and help us lead the learning of others.

The International Reading Association (now the International Literacy Association) provides standards to guide our work. Standard Six, Professional Learning and Leadership, is particularly relevant to our work as coaches. This standard focuses on celebrating the culture of lifelong learning in schools by creating collaborative learning experiences and effective professional development for teachers:

Scan the QR code to read the most up-to-date version of International Literacy Association's standards for specialized literacy professionals.
http://bit.ly/2AB2Rti

ORGANIZATIONS AND COMMUNITIES

International Literacy Association	http://literacyworldwide.org
National Council for Teachers of English	www.ncte.org
Choice Literacy	www.choiceliteracy.com
Lead Literacy	www.leadliteracy.com
The Educator Collaborative	https://theeducatorcollaborative.com
Literacy in Learning Exchange	www2.ncte.org/blog/2015/09/the-literacy-in-learning-exchange/
Heinemann PLC Series	www.heinemann.com/blog/category/plc-series/

Figure 3.1: *Organizations and communities that support professional learning*

❋ Effective professional learning is evidence based in ways that reflect both competent and critical use of relevant research and is thoughtfully planned, ongoing, differentiated, and embedded in the work of all faculty members.

❋ Effective professional learning is inclusive and collaborative across parents or guardians, the community, and all school staff, including education support personnel, classroom teachers, specialized personnel, supervisors, and administrators.

❋ Effective professional learning is focused on content determined by careful consideration and assessment of the needs of students, teachers, parents or guardians, and the larger community of stakeholders.

❋ Effective professional learning is supportive of the need for instruction that is responsive to the range of diversity.

❋ Effective professional learning is grounded in research related to adult learning and organizational change as well as research on reading acquisition, development, assessment, and instruction.

❋ Effective professional learning in schools requires collaboration, is job embedded, builds trust, and empowers teachers, and those who lead such efforts must have effective interpersonal, leadership, and communication skills. (International Reading Association 2010)

Why do these standards matter so much to the work we do? Literacy coaches lead the learning of the teachers they work with, who then lead the learning of their students. We must ensure our learning experiences for teachers mirror best practices for the classroom. By crafting meaningful learning experiences for teachers, we engage their hearts and minds. By providing them with useful, relevant, and meaningful instructional resources tailored to their interests and needs, they strengthen the learning of their students. By innovating our professional development, we inspire innovative literacy learning in the classroom. Leading the learning of others is important. It has the potential to transform the classroom with the work we do. Instruction infused with technology is not about learning new tools and apps; it is about transforming our knowledge, understandings, and practices through those very tools. Digital tools invite participation and collaboration throughout the learning process; make learning relevant, meaningful, and con- nected; and inspire change for the classroom. Figure 3.2 outlines the possible ways our traditional methods of professional development might expand with the use of digital tools.

WITHOUT TECHNOLOGY, Coaches and Teachers . . .	WITH TECHNOLOGY, Coaches and Teachers . . .
Create on-site professional development sessions after school and on conference days with colleagues.	Increase participation and engagement in professional development sessions with digital and back-channel tools.
Find and save books, curriculum materials, and resources to use with teachers.	Digitally find and curate materials, curriculum, and resources with digital bookshelves and bulletin boards.
Copy and share documents and lesson materials for teachers.	Curate documents and other materials digitally.
Work individually with teachers for personalized coaching and learning.	Digitally create guided lessons, tutorials, and interactive documents on pertinent literacy learning topics for teachers.
Attend local, state, and national professional development and learning opportunities.	Meet with literacy professionals virtually and attend literacy conferences and sessions through digital means.

Figure 3.2: *Literacy coaching activities with and without technology*

How do you learn best? Are you able to pick up a new skill after only reading about how to complete it? Or do you need to watch a demonstration before you feel comfortable enough to try it yourself? Can you easily take responsibility for your own learning without any outside accountability? Or do you need the gentle reminders and expectations of others to motivate your continued efforts? Every learner has different strengths, needs, and preferences for learning. Literacy coaches must attend to those varied needs and celebrate the multiple dimensions of learning. Digital tools provide access, engagement, and resources to fuel teacher learning. In addition to providing professional texts for teachers, we might direct them to a collection of articles or digital texts on a selected topic. Rather than create a traditional PowerPoint presentation, we might catch teachers' attention by using a more dynamic platform, such as Prezi. Figure 3.3 offers suggestions for digitally enhancing the tools we use to create teacher learning experiences.

TRADITIONAL TOOLS for Professional Development	DIGITAL TOOLS for Professional Development
PowerPoint presentations	Multimodal, interactive presentations
Small-group discussions and problem solving	Digital and virtual discussions and back-channel conversations
In-person learning activities	Videos and tutorials provided in a "flipped" coaching model
Conversational tools (discussion, sticky notes, chart paper)	Microwriting and reflection through social media

Figure 3.3: *Traditional literacy coaching tools and digital transformations*

Design Inviting Professional Development

Literacy coaches design and deliver professional development in multiple settings to teachers: whole faculty, small collaborative groups, and individual coaching. Think about a recent, positive learning experience you had. What made you define that experience as an engaging and successful one? Chances are that experience was something you chose, was relevant to your interests and needs, kept you engaged and motivated, and made you feel competent and successful. If designed effectively with the needs of teachers and adult learners in mind, professional development extends teachers' knowledge on a given topic and inspires connections to the classroom.

We can create guidance for ourselves as literacy coaches to ensure that the professional development we offer to teachers is meaningful, engaging, and relevant to their teaching lives. Here are some of my guidelines:

1. The learning experiences you provide must model those you hope for in the classroom. We can't tell teachers to do one thing, but engage in another.

2. Make learning relevant. Build on teachers' knowledge, interests, and experiences and ensure the time spent together is worthwhile.

3. Connect, engage, and inspire. Involve teachers in all aspects of professional development and encourage varied forms of participation throughout.

4. Continue the conversations. Blur the boundaries of bounded learning sessions and create opportunities for continued collaboration.

5. Connect to the classroom. Professional development sessions are starting points for learning. The real learning happens in the classroom when we use our knowledge to better support student learning.

Technology and digital tools can help differentiate the professional development we provide teachers, ignite our presentations, increase teacher engagement, and provide useful resources for inspired teaching.

Digitally Differentiate Professional Development

A few years ago, I was asked to deliver a keynote address to a group of reading coaches working in local schools. I created a presentation that focused on reading motivation, choosing books for students, strategy teaching, and the importance of teacher language. I even involved social media and live participation. I was quite pleased with how it turned out and was looking forward to my session. That all changed when I arrived. Imagine my surprise when I realized my audience was not a group of reading coaches, but seniors who listen to students read. Although they were very attentive and polite, the content I shared with them was not targeted to their needs or their technology prowess. They were not teaching reading, but listening to reading. They were not instructing, but connecting with kids. I could have crafted a very different presentation that would have better prepared them for their experiences ahead. I left that session feeling very defeated and apologetic for not knowing my audience. From then on, I vowed to get to know my audience's needs and ensure a worthwhile and meaningful experience for participants. Technology can help us do just that.

Start by learning more about the teachers you work with. When we know more, we can do better and ensure that our coaching is a good fit for each teacher. Small things, seemingly outside of our content coaching, can make a big impact. Teachers know when you take the time to get to know them. Remembering to bring hard candies to your session for the teacher who does not prefer chocolate (I know, there are only a few out there!) will be appreciated. Commenting on a beautiful dress or sweater means you noticed them. Asking about a teacher's child who was sick a few days ago shows you care. These small acknowledgments help teachers connect with you and lead to more substantive coaching connections later on. Figure 3.4 provides a list of things you might want to learn about each teacher you work with.

THINGS TO DISCOVER ABOUT THE TEACHERS YOU WORK WITH

Interests, hobbies, family, and friends

Reading and writing lives

Instructional strengths and needs

Classroom preferences and ideas (management, routines, etc.)

Preferred ways of communicating

Plans and goals for the future

Figure 3.4: *Useful things to know about the teachers you coach*

Although good old-fashioned conversations are a staple coaching tool, digital survey tools, such as Google Forms, can help you discover exactly what your teachers need and want for their own professional learning.

BE A TECHSPERT

BEGINNING

TECH TOOL

GOOGLE FORMS: *A tool to create and analyze surveys*
WEBSITE: *www.google.com/forms/about/*
COST: *Free!*
TECHSPERT LEVEL: *Great for beginning tech users*

Begin with the planning process and survey teachers on the kinds of topics they would like to explore in your professional development sessions together over the coming school year. Ideally, teachers would link their names to their responses so you can learn more about each teacher and craft a professional development plan that meets their needs. Yet, anonymity can be powerful and teachers might honestly respond more readily if they can do so anonymously. Figure 3.5 shows a screenshot of a portion of a completed survey.

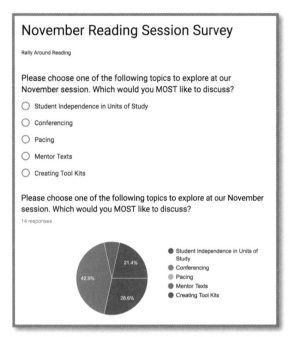

November Reading Session Survey

Rally Around Reading

Please choose one of the following topics to explore at our November session. Which would you MOST like to discuss?

○ Student Independence in Units of Study

○ Conferencing

○ Pacing

○ Mentor Texts

○ Creating Tool Kits

Please choose one of the following topics to explore at our November session. Which would you MOST like to discuss?

14 responses

- Student Independence in Units of Study
- Conferencing
- Pacing
- Mentor Texts
- Creating Tool Kits

21.4%
42.9%
28.6%

Figure 3.5: *Google survey form and results to support planning for future professional development*

You can also use digital tools to create entrance and exit tickets for teachers within your professional development sessions. You'll gather information that will immediately inform your work. At the start of a session, ask teachers to complete a quick survey or questionnaire. You might ask them to rate their understanding of a topic, such as running records, or to submit a question they hope is answered within the session. If you use a tool like Google Forms, results can be aggregated and displayed immediately for group reflection. Figure 3.6 shows the results of an entrance ticket for a professional development session.

You might also create brief exit tickets after a session is complete. These exit tickets might focus on the content learned during the session, ask for feedback on the usefulness of the activities, or request information about how teachers might use their new knowledge in the classroom. Teachers can also submit any lingering questions they have so that you can address them in a follow-up email or shared session notes. See Figure 3.7 for an example.

Want to take it a step further? Try using video tools to have teachers reflect on their own learning and share ideas with other teachers. Using a tool like Flipgrid, a video response and reflection app, teachers can quickly and easily record video reflections on their learning and share them with you. You can reflect on these responses later to inform your next session together.

BE A TECHSPERT

BEGINNING

TECH TOOL

FLIPGRID: *A video discussion tool*
WEBSITE: *https://info.flipgrid.com*
COST: *Free! Premium plans vary.*
TECHSPERT LEVEL: *Great for beginning tech users*

Leading Literacy Survey

What best describes your role in schools?

○ Classroom Teacher

○ Literacy Specialist

○ Administrator

○ Professional Development Provider

○ Other

In what ways do you support teacher learning? Check all that apply.

☐ Lead professional development sessions

☐ Provide literacy coaching

☐ Facilitate book studies or grade level meetings

☐ Lead data team meetings

☐ Provide materials and resources

☐ Make curriculum and assessment decisions

What best describes your role in schools?

20 responses

- Classroom Teacher
- Literacy Specialist
- Administrator
- Professional Development Provider
- Other

Running Record Exit Ticket

Which best characterizes how you feel right now?

○ I need more practice and guidance coding running records

○ I am ready to analyze my results

On a scale of 1-5, how comfortable do you feel determining a student's independent vs. instructional level?

1	2	3	4	5
○	○	○	○	○

On a scale of 1-5, how comfortable do you feel determining a student's independent vs. instructional level?

1	2	3	4	5
○	○	○	○	○

On a scale of 1-5, how comfortable do you feel talking to students' families about reading levels?

1	2	3	4	5
○	○	○	○	○

Figure 3.6 (left): *Survey form and results from a survey used to inform a professional development session*

Figure 3.7 (above): *An exit ticket created by Krista Senatore for a professional development session on running records*

LAUNCHING POINT ✳

What is the next professional development session you are planning? Create a brief three-question survey to send to teachers before your session. You might ask them to rate how comfortable they feel discussing the topic, ask for their preferences in session activities, or share a question they hope will be answered in the session. Send the survey to teachers and use the results to inform your planning.

Each piece of information gathered from teachers can inform your practice and ensure your collaborations are authentic, relevant, and timely. Use this information beyond your professional development sessions and in your individual coaching as well: suggest books, mentor texts, articles, websites, and even other teachers that could fuel teacher's interests and inquiries in meaningful and authentic ways. These connections pave the way for more sustained, intentional, and collaborative work.

Inspired by the possibilities to personalize the curriculum that digital surveys provide, Joyce, a fifth-grade teacher, decided to give it a try in her classroom and surveyed her students on their interests for an upcoming unit of study in reading. Initially, she planned to use reading passages to model close reading skills and evidence-based reading responses on a variety of topics. After seeing how easy it was to gain rich information through Google Forms, she decided to bring her students into the planning process and learn more about what they wanted to read. Her students answered brief questions about their reading habits and interests. With that information, she tailored a close reading collection to their interests and hobbies rather than simply practicing close reading skills through a random collection of passages. A screenshot of the survey and students' responses are seen in Figure 3.8.

Her students were more engaged and she was pleased with the level of interest and the volume of reading, reinforcing her ideas about how important choice and ownership are in the learning process. She continues to use Google Forms to learn more about her students to inform her instruction.

What Do You Want to Explore?

* Required

What would you most like to read about from the list below? *
- Inventions and Inventors
- Gaming
- Animals
- Weather
- Sports
- Holidays

What other topics would you like to read about from the list below? *
- Inventions and Inventors
- Gaming
- Animals
- Weather
- Sports
- Holidays

What topics would you like to read about that were not on the list?

Your answer

What would you most like to read about from the list below?

20 responses

- Inventions and Inventors
- Gaming
- Animals
- Weather
- Sports
- Holidays

25%
10%
10%
10%
40%

Figure 3.8: *A survey form designed to learn more about students' reading preferences, and resulting responses*

Reimagine Presentations with Multimodal Tools

Just about all of us can identify a time when we had to endure a learning experience that was less than optimal: boring lecture-type sessions with basic, canned presentations. Professional development needs to excite the mind and engage the senses. It needs to appeal to all kinds of learners with different preferences and modalities for learning. Literacy in today's times is more than text. It includes multiple literacies and multimodalities with text, graphics, and hyperlinks. So why would we teach teachers about literacy instruction using anything less? Technology and digital tools can help us reimagine our presentations to shift our thinking about literacy, engage with others, and ignite teacher learning.

Memes are an excellent way to engage teachers and prompt reflection. A meme is a narrative reflection with a graphic representation to anchor our thinking and inspire our work. Memes remind you of what is important and what you are working toward. The memes in Figure 3.9 are posted in my office and remind me what is most important in my work with teachers and students.

Although memes are great reflection tools, they have also provided me with a rule of thumb for creating presentations: less is more and graphics inspire. Rather than fill up PowerPoint slides full of text and too much literal information, I think critically and carefully about what I want teachers to ponder and consider. I then create a slide around that idea, rather than the details surrounding it. I let the meme be the starting point of the conversation and follow the lead of my teachers, adding in needed details and information as the conversation evolves. This kind of slide typically garners more discussion and critical thinking than a page of concrete facts and information can. Figure 3.10 provides multiple tools to easily create inspiring memes for your sessions.

As a personal rule of thumb when creating my own professional development sessions, I pair text with pictures, audio, and/or video clips that illustrate a shared concept. This drives the

Figure 3.9: *Inspiring memes for literacy teaching and learning*

MULTIMODAL AND GRAPHIC TOOLS	
Wordle	www.wordle.net
Tagxedo	www.tagxedo.com
Notography	https://notography.com
Canva	www.canva.com
Recite	http://recite.com
PixTeller	http://pixteller.com

Figure 3.10: *Tools to create memes and graphics for professional development*

conversation forward, yet grounds it in real classroom scenarios. Are you focused on refining your guided reading small groups in the classroom? Show a video of an effective guided reading lesson and then plan a lesson for one of your teacher's groups. Are you examining close reading in the classroom? After engaging in an actual close read of a text together, view a classroom doing the same and make connections across experiences.

LAUNCHING POINT
✳

Let's have a go at creating a meme to inspire your coaching. Maybe you feel like you are not artistic enough, or creative enough. Don't worry! The digital tool provides the art and creativity; you just need to provide the text and create a layout that works for you! Go ahead and give it a try. Start by identifying the text you want to include. What phrase inspires you? Next, choose a tool to try. I suggest using Recite or Pixteller as an easy starting point. Choose a graphic and paste your text into the meme. Voila!

Promote Teacher Engagement with Digital Tools

We can have the best presentation under the best circumstances, but if we do not plan to actively engage teachers throughout the learning process, our work is moot and our efforts in vain. We already discussed how to create digital entrance and exit tickets using Google Forms within our professional development. But why not use them as digital status of the class updates throughout your sessions as well? Take a quick read of the audience and keep your pulse on the learning by asking teachers to check in with you. Create quick, one-question surveys that teachers can easily complete by scanning a QR code with a mobile device. Or, shorten a URL for teachers to type into their browsers using https://goo.gl/. You might ask teachers to anonymously note if they would like continued practice with a particular skill or instructional idea or if they are ready to move on. You can ask teachers to rate their understanding of a concept to gauge need for further practice. Or, ask teachers to pose a challenge they need to overcome in the classroom to continue their learning. You might even ask teachers to pose questions that they need answered before moving on.

Because these surveys are anonymous, teachers can be honest in their reflections. Figure 3.11 provides an example of a check-in designed for a session on making instructional decisions for guided reading.

While privately reflecting on the results is useful in planning your future work with teachers, publicly displaying the results for teachers to see immediately in your session promotes conversation and demonstrates how to use data to inform our teaching in the classroom as well.

You might also try Padlet to capture the thinking of the group. Throughout your sessions, encourage teachers to share their thinking on a Padlet wall. This may be free thinking, resources to share, or responses to specific questions. Just as we would stop to reflect on a shared topic in conversation, teachers can note their thinking on a digital wall. In one professional development session I cofacilitated with another literacy coach, Logan Fisher and I had teachers write their thinking on sticky notes to share with the group. We also encouraged teachers to contribute digital sticky notes as well, for those comfortable doing so. We combined both into a shared reference (see Figure 3.12) and used it as a tool to guide our next session. This thinking was displayed instantly in real time, and the audience could easily and quickly see all shared contributions.

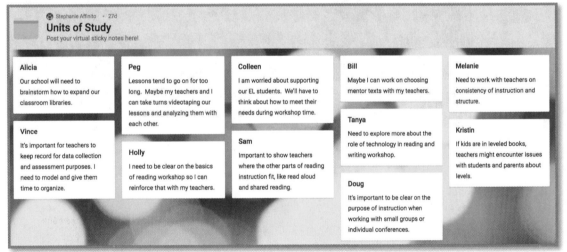

Guided Reading Check In

Please complete this break check-in to inform the rest of our session together.

How comfortable do you feel using the Continuum on a scale of 1 - 5?

| | 1 | 2 | 3 | 4 | 5 | |
Not very comfortable ○ ○ ○ ○ ○ Very comfortable

Would you like additional practice with a sample student and reading conference?

○ Yes
○ No

Figure 3.11: *A quick check-in survey form for teachers in a guided reading professional development session*

Figure 3.12: *A Padlet wall representing ideas generated in a professional development session*

Sometimes, we all need a little help to capture teachers' attention in our sessions. A quick movie clip, a funny comic, or an unexpected activity can quickly gain teachers' attention, break the ice, and get everyone motivated for the learning to come. I have collected many over time as my go-to resources. Scan the QR code to view my Padlet wall. Have any to add? Please share!

Scan the QR code to view my icebreakers and hands-on activities for professional development.
http://bit.ly/2zYO9Ji

It is essential to involve teachers in their own learning from the initial planning stages to the reflection after your sessions. When we feel engaged and involved, we have an energy for learning that is contagious. Every conversation, interaction, and experience is an opportunity to learn and think about our practice. Rather than limit our learning and conversation to the confines of a bounded session or location, we can continue to engage with teachers when they are back in their classrooms, creating back channels for discussion. Back channels are unofficial channels of communication that begin before, continue during, and remain available after professional development sessions.

Here are a few ideas to try:

1. Consider using a formal back-channel tool, such as TodaysMeet. During a session, teachers access the site through a URL address and can instantly and easily add ideas, post questions, and even link to websites to engage with others.

BE A TECHSPERT

BEGINNING

TECH TOOL

TODAYSMEET: *A back channel for conversation*
WEBSITE: *https://todaysmeet.com*
COST: *Free!*
TECHSPERT LEVEL: *Great for beginning tech users*

As a coach, you can easily integrate these comments into your in-person conversations and help continue the learning when the session is complete. Figure 3.13 offers an example of a TodaysMeet session.

2. End each professional development session with an invitation to continue the learning together. Pose a question or suggestion for reflection with an avenue for conversation. You might ask

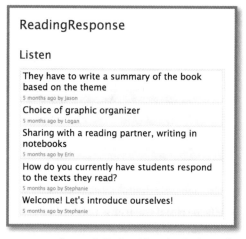

ReadingResponse

Listen

They have to write a summary of the book based on the theme
5 months ago by Jason

Choice of graphic organizer
5 months ago by Logan

Sharing with a reading partner, writing in notebooks
5 months ago by Erin

How do you currently have students respond to the texts they read?
5 months ago by Stephanie

Welcome! Let's introduce ourselves!
5 months ago by Stephanie

Figure 3.13: *A sample TodaysMeet back channel*

teachers to tweet ideas to your school hashtag, post questions to your literacy Facebook page, or contribute to a shared document created in your session.

3. Send out session minutes or your own reflections from a professional development session and encourage conversation and collaboration. Using Google Docs is especially useful for this because teachers can either add their own reflections in a shared document or add comments for others to consider. See Figure 3.14 for an example.

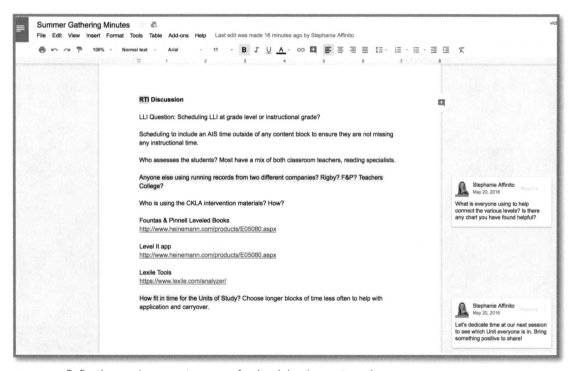

Figure 3.14: *Reflections and comments on a professional development session*

LAUNCHING POINT ✳

Choose one of the ideas shared for creating a back channel for your teachers and try it with your teachers this week. Don't be discouraged if teachers do not immediately respond. It takes a few experiences with something new to be comfortable enough to try it. Capitalize on participation and don't give up! Keep trying or choose another method to encourage your teachers to participate.

Leverage the power of back-channel conversation and use it to inform and continue professional learning. When we sustain dialogue with teachers, it ensures their learning will transfer into the classroom to impact students.

Flip Literacy Coaching for Personalized Learning

Typically, professional development time with teachers is precious and never quite long enough to accomplish everything we had planned. As coaches, we can use technology and digital tools to flip our literacy coaching and ensure the time spent together with teachers is worthwhile: discussing, sharing, innovating, and applying new learning to the classroom. Flipped learning is a pedagogical approach where individual reflection precedes group collaboration and discussion. Learners prepare for upcoming learning experiences by reading, viewing videos and tutorials, and reflecting on their own learning. Then, they "come to class" ready to discuss and engage with the content, grapple with uncertainties, and apply their learning.

In a flipped coaching model, teachers personalize their learning with guided lessons and tutorials meant to build content and pedagogical knowledge. Teachers can then access and engage with these resources any time. This frees up time in our often-too-short professional development sessions to work with that knowledge, rather than simply transmit it. There are a few ways we can immediately apply these principles to our work as literacy coaches:

1. Create guided lessons and tutorials as on-demand resources for teachers. Use audio, video, and other digital tools to share content with teachers before professional development sessions and to have on-demand for later learning and review.

2. Create interactive documents to personalize and differentiate teacher learning. Use QR codes and ThingLink to differentiate your coaching content and create useful resources for teaching. (Read more about ThingLink on page 85).

3. Cultivate digital portfolios of instructional resources and practices. Give teachers access to high-quality classrooms filled with effective literacy practices to easily envision what they might look like in their own classrooms.

Intrigued? Keep reading for some ideas to try in your coaching tomorrow!

Create Guided Lessons and Tutorials

There are multiple digital tools that can help flip your coaching. I rely on screencasting tools and interactive whiteboards to support my work, but you should choose the type of tool based on your purpose for coaching. If you want to give teachers background information on a topic that you will discuss in an upcoming professional development session, you might choose screencasting tools. Screencasting tools, such as Screencast-O-Matic, provide a digital recording of your computer screen's output.

TECH TOOL

SCREENCAST-O-MATIC: *Online screencasting tool*
WEBSITE: *https://screencast-o-matic.com*
COST: *Free! Premium plans vary.*
TECHSPERT LEVEL: *Great for beginning tech users*

These quick videos not only can provide teachers with important information before your sessions, but also can ignite excitement for an upcoming session and provide incentives for their viewing. For example, if you are working to level classroom libraries, you might narrate a presentation on the tools available for such work and then actually level books during your time together. Or, if you are exploring nonfiction text features with teachers, you might create a brief presentation on the different types of text features and then spend your in-person time creating lessons to use with students.

Interactive whiteboards allow users to annotate, animate, and narrate lessons for both teachers and students. If you want to provide teachers with a concrete example of an instructional practice, choose digital tools that not only record your computer screen, but allow you to interact with the content. I prefer Educreations or Explain Everything for my work.

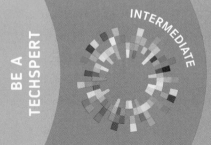

TECH TOOL

EDUCREATIONS: *A recordable, interactive whiteboard*
WEBSITE: *www.educreations.com*
COST: *Free! Premium plans vary.*
TECHSPERT LEVEL: *Good for intermediate tech users*

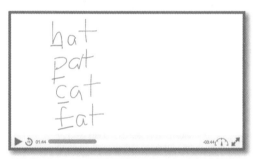

Figure 3.15: *A brief tutorial on creating effective word-building routines*

LITERACY COACHING EASY BUTTONS

Navigate a curriculum website.

Navigate an assessment website.

Use a particular tool or program within your district.

Show how to contribute to shared curriculum documents.

Show how to complete response to intervention documents.

Figure 3.16: *Possible literacy coaching easy buttons*

Using these tools, I model word work routines, interactive writing, close reading annotation, and more. For example, if you want to model a word work routine, you could create a video through Educreations, recording both your actions and your audio as a model, as shown in Figure 3.15.

If you want to explore close reading, you could read and annotate a text "live" for teachers as an example and then create close reading lessons for the classroom during your professional development sessions.

You might also use these flipped coaching resources as your "easy" button in coaching. I know there are things you find yourself saying over and over again or things you demonstrate over and over again; you wish there was a better way. There is. Record yourself saying or doing these things and make them available to teachers on demand. You might demonstrate how to access a district curriculum or assessment website, how to navigate a district shared space, or how to use a particular digital tool. Stop and think for a moment. What would your easy button say and do if you had one? Figure 3.16 lists a few that I created or have seen used by other coaches.

Because you may find yourself with a collection of flipped coaching lessons, you'll need to house your creations in an easy-to-access space. It does no good to create coaching lessons and tutorials if teachers cannot easily access them when they need them most. Link to them on your school website, create a shared Google Folder, or even link to them to your Google+ Community page. Curate your resources in an easily sharable format to encourage personalized teacher learning, just as teachers might for their own students.

LAUNCHING POINT ✳

Ah, I know your wheels are turning! I imagine you have more than a few ideas for how you might flip your literacy coaching, so go ahead and give it a try. You might start with an easy button. Record a screencast of yourself engaging in something that your teachers might need a tutorial for. Do not expect perfection on the first try at all! Keep it real and teachers will respond more readily. I rarely rerecord my flipped coaching resources, even if I make a mistake, because it shows teachers that we all make mistakes and move on. Do you feel like sharing your first flipped coaching resource to inspire another reader to give it a try? Send a tweet to @AffinitoLit to share with other readers!

CONNECTION TO THE CLASSROOM ✳

Inspired by how Educreations provided narration to the writing and illustrations in the tutorials, a group of kindergarten teachers decided to use Educreations to strengthen their writing instruction. Admittedly a bit hesitant about how five-year-olds would manage the new technology, their fears were quickly calmed as the students eagerly wrote and discussed their writing. At the end of the introductory lesson, I shared that I created an anchor chart of the steps for creating a writing video. One five-year-old quickly said, "I do not think we need the chart, Mrs. A, but I think Mrs. M does!" We all had a good laugh and realized what was holding us back was our fear that students would have difficulty managing the digital tools, not the students' abilities. In fact, they produced amazing pieces of writing in that session and continue to do so, because Educreations has become a staple tool in their classroom. See Figure 3.17 for an example.

Figure 3.17: *Sample use of Educreations in an elementary classroom*

Create Interactive Documents

Interactive documents add another layer of engagement to your sessions. They make documents come alive with text, audio, video, and hyperlinks. These documents link teachers to useful resources and provide access and differentiated support for their learning. QR codes and ThingLink offer numerous possibilities to extend teacher learning and encourage interaction.

QR codes can quickly and easily enhance any professional development session and give teachers immediate access to information or interactive session activities. By bringing them into your professional development sessions, teachers can easily and quickly scan the codes to link to materials, websites, or activities. They can instantly access articles and blogs for reading and discussion, complete a quick survey on their learning to guide the session, or contribute to a collective document/bulletin board and share their thinking and resources with others.

Because I teach literacy classes online, it can be challenging to teach particular concepts, such as running records, to new teachers. How do you teach running records to a group of teachers you will never see or talk to in person? It can be a daunting task, but one made easier with QR codes. To support practice in coding and analyzing running records, I created interactive documents to help teachers practice and check their skills. See Figure 3.18 for an example.

Teachers choose a running record to complete and print out the text of the book to follow along. The QR code on the bottom of the page links teachers directly to an audio or video file of a child reading that very text. Teachers listen to the recording and practice their coding skills on a separate piece of paper. Once complete, they analyze the running record and complete their calculations. Teachers scan the second QR code linked to a completed version of the same running record, compare their results, and reflect on their performance. Figure 3.19 lists a few ways you might use QR codes in your professional development sessions with teachers.

Figure 3.18: *An interactive running record tutorial*

WAYS TO USE QR CODES IN PROFESSIONAL DEVELOPMENT	EXAMPLE
Provide teachers with a link to your presentation.	
Link to digital entrance and exit tickets.	
Link to digital bulletin board or back channel to capture the thinking of the group.	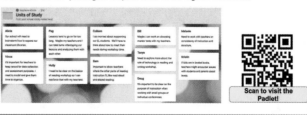

Figure 3.19: *Ways to use QR codes in professional development*   *(continues)*

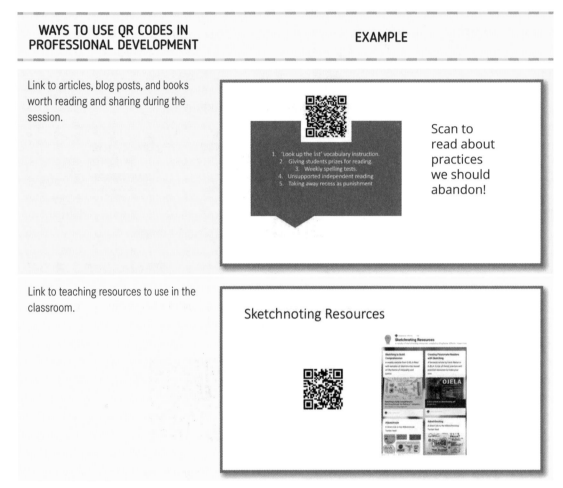

WAYS TO USE QR CODES IN PROFESSIONAL DEVELOPMENT	EXAMPLE
Link to articles, blog posts, and books worth reading and sharing during the session.	
Link to teaching resources to use in the classroom.	

Figure 3.19: *Ways to use QR codes in professional development (continued)*

You might also use QR codes to enhance book studies and lesson documents. For example, you might link to your recorded book introduction of a professional library text. Add the QR code right to the cover of the book or paste a QR code to the digital resources for the book inside the front cover. Be creative in your thinking about how QR codes might support your work. Figure 3.20 lists additional possibilities for using QR codes in your coaching.

WAYS TO USE QR CODES IN LITERACY COACHING

Provide book recommendations to teachers.

Link to study group questions on texts in a book study.

Use as models in your coaching space.

Use for unexpected reading and other school initiatives, such as IMWAYR.

Link to websites and resources in professional development.

Link to exit, entrance, and check-ins during professional development.

Link to videos and manuals directly on curriculum documents.

Link to flipped coaching tutorials and lessons.

Figure 3.20: *Ideas for how to use QR codes in literacy coaching*

CONNECTION TO THE CLASSROOM

Inspired by the simple yet creative use of QR codes to listen to students reading during running records, a few teachers decided to transfer their learning to their own classrooms. In one school, teachers worked together to record themselves reading children's books in their classroom library using audioBoom and Vocaroo.

Figure 3.21: *A picture of a QR code inside a new listening station book*

They linked the audio recordings to QR codes and taped them into their classroom library books (see Figure 3.21). Students could easily scan the QR code with a mobile device for an instant listening station, one with fewer technology difficulties than previously used in the past. Teachers did not need to purchase recordings and were not limited in the books used in their listening stations, because any book could easily be turned into an audio recording.

The teachers created a shared Google Drive Folder to share additional recordings. Each time a teacher created a recording, they shared it and added the QR code to the drive so it would be accessible to all. They even involved other school faculty. The principal, special teachers, and other school staff recorded themselves reading books and added those recordings to the Google Drive. The literacy specialist also had her upper elementary students practice their fluency skills in an authentic manner by recording books and linking them to QR codes to share with primary classrooms.

BE A TECHSPERT

BEGINNING

TECH TOOL

AUDIOBOOM: *A tool to record and share content online*
WEBSITE: *https://audioboom.com*
COST: *Free!*
TECHSPERT LEVEL: *Great for beginning tech users*

BE A TECHSPERT

BEGINNING

TECH TOOL

VOCAROO: *Online voice recording service*
WEBSITE: *http://vocaroo.com*
COST: *Free!*
TECHSPERT LEVEL: *Great for beginning tech users*

QR codes are wonderful coaching tools, but there are even more interactive tools available to help inspire our coaching and teaching. ThingLink is a tool that links websites, files, and audio to a single, interactive document.

TECH TOOL

THINGLINK: *A tool to annotate videos and images*
WEBSITE: *www.thinglink.com*
COST: *Free! Premium plans vary.*
TECHSPERT LEVEL: *Best for advanced tech users*

I have used ThingLink in multiple ways, but one of my favorite ways is to showcase effective literacy classrooms and link to the tools needed to create them. Figure 3.22 provides an example of an interactive image I made to support the creation of classroom word walls.

By using ThingLink, the image not only provides a vision for what a word wall might look like, it gives teachers the tools they need to create it. So, how did I do it? First, I found a picture of a word wall to use as an example. I recommend mining your own school to take snapshots of the amazing literacy spaces you find, but if you need to, you can always use permissible online photos. Next, I linked important resources to the picture: descriptions and reflective questions, articles that help teachers think through key practices (such as which words to use and why), and websites with helpful ideas and resources. As teachers view the picture, they can follow the links that speak to them most, based on their interest and area of need. I shared the completed ThingLink with teachers as part of a professional development session on word walls.

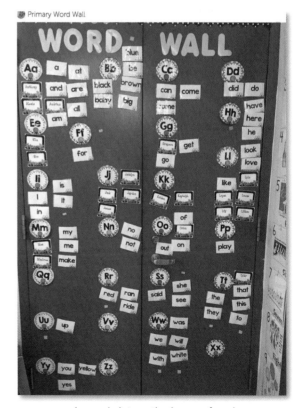

Figure 3.22: *A sample interactive image of a primary classroom word wall*

Some teachers were most interested in exploring the basic ideas behind using word walls. Others were interested in making their word wall more interactive, and others wanted to learn new word wall activities to try with their class. These personal webquests put teachers in charge of their own learning. Figure 3.23 outlines a list of possible ThingLinks you might create, but any picture of a classroom area or instructional routine could turn into an interactive document to inspire teacher learning. The possibilities are endless.

Why not simply use a collection of curated sites on classroom libraries? By starting with an image, teachers can easily envision the practice in their classroom. By linking to various resources, they can quickly find materials based on their interests. As teachers interact, they typically find additional resources and items to add to the ThingLink. Continue to revise and add to these interactive documents based on the feedback you receive so that you have a collaborative representation of your coaching work.

POSSIBLE THINGLINKS FOR LITERACY COACHING

Classroom libraries

Literacy stations

Word walls

Guided reading spaces

Morning check-in stations

Whole-group teaching areas

Reading and writing notebooks

Figure 3.23: *Ways to use ThingLink in literacy coaching*

LAUNCHING POINT ✳

Start exploring the possibilities for ThingLink. Before you create your own, browse the many ThingLinks that already exist. Visit www.thinglink.com /edu and get inspired! Next, create your own free account and have a go at creating your own. Start small and take a picture of a classroom space you want to celebrate. Link to three resources you think your teachers will find helpful, and share it in an upcoming professional development session.

Support Instructional Innovations

As literacy coaches, we have the luxury of visiting multiple classrooms within a school, schools, or even a district. We see innovative instruction, find ideas for classroom management and setup, learn new ideas to engage students, and view beautiful displays of student learning. When we visit classrooms, we widen our thinking, gain new perspectives on learning, and, simply put, collect amazing ideas to use in our work. When I visit schools, I typically collect ideas in a note-book. Similar to a writer's notebook, I jot notes about my thinking, sketch ideas for the classroom, and plant seeds for future blog posts so I can share my learning with others. More recently, I have a notes page on my phone to quickly capture my ideas and often take quick pictures (with permission, of course).

Teachers rarely have the opportunity to visit other classrooms and schools. As a literacy coach, you can take your experiences and make them visible and accessible to all. Document the instructional innovations you see across the classrooms in which you work. Take pictures of your lessons and artifacts of student learning. Record short video clips of your lessons. Snap pictures of wall displays, literacy stations, small-group teaching spaces, and helpful mentor charts. Take pictures of small-group instruction, whole-group read-alouds, and short instructional routines to help teachers visualize a world outside of their own classrooms. Share these gems though Google Drive, on your Google+ Community, your own protected website, or a Padlet wall. Shelley Fenton uses Google+ Communities to highlight innovative teaching practices. She posts pictures of classrooms, gives kudos to teachers trying new techniques, and encourages interaction. Figure 3.24 provides examples of her work.

 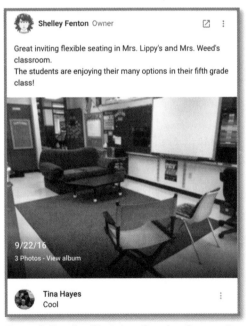

Figure 3.24: *Screenshots of celebratory posts in Shelley Fenton's Reading Workshop Google+ Community*

These mentor images and videos are critical to our learning and fuel a collegial atmosphere where ideas are valued and freely shared in the spirit of teacher collaboration. Over time and practice, continue to add pictures and video clips of the instruction you see as you visit classrooms. It will help teachers live vicariously through you and the work you do. Start by curating these shared resources and then invite teachers to contribute and collaboratively create them.

LAUNCHING POINT ✳

> *Think about a moment in your coaching when you wished all your teachers could see the same thing. Perhaps it was a particularly effective anchor chart or a beautiful display of student work. Make a point to take a picture or video of the innovation and share it with your teachers in some way. You might post it on your digital community page, email it to your teachers, or display it in your next professional development session. Just be sure to get the teacher's permission first, and if student work is included, ensure it is only posted to a password-protected site with administrator permission.*

Digitally Curate Shared Resources

A quick glance at my desk and my dining room table reveals multiple piles. They may seem random and askew, but each has an important purpose: books to read, papers to save, materials I need for my next class. As teachers, we accumulate and juggle a great deal of stuff: curriculum documents, assessment materials, instructional materials, collections of websites, and more. Social bookmarking sites, such as Diigo, Symbaloo, Pinterest, and Padlet allow us to curate our most treasured resources in list or graphic form and provide easier access to the many ideas you share.

There are many options for curating your online curriculum resources, depending on your preferences. First, choose your format. If you prefer your resources in list form, choose a tool such as Diigo. If you prefer graphic visuals, choose Symbaloo. If you want to easily share and comment on other lists, choose Padlet or Pinterest. Let your needs and preferences guide your tool choice.

BE A TECHSPERT

BEGINNING

TECH TOOL

DIIGO: *A social bookmarking website*
WEBSITE: *www.diigo.com*
COST: *Free! Premium plans vary.*
TECHSPERT LEVEL: *Great for beginning tech users*

BE A TECHSPERT

BEGINNING

TECH TOOL

SYMBALOO: *A social bookmarking site*
WEBSITE: *www.symbaloo.com*
COST: *Free!*
TECHSPERT LEVEL: *Great for beginning tech users*

BE A TECHSPERT

BEGINNING

TECH TOOL

PINTEREST: *A social networking site through virtual bulletin boards*
WEBSITE: *www.pinterest.com*
COST: *Free!*
TECHSPERT LEVEL: *Great for beginning tech users*

Figures 3.25, 3.26, 3.27, and 3.28 offer four examples of my collections.

Upgrade lists to outliners

564 items total, 2 unread   Filter:All ⬍   ⬆Collapse   Date Updated ⬍

Tags (30)   Top ⬍

Untagged	553
Firefox	5
Mozilla	4
google	2
blended	2
LERN	1
Diigo	1
ELA	1
examples	1
blog	1
blended learning	1
GoogleEDU	1
information	1
information lite...	1
ira	1
difference	1

View tag cloud »

My Lists (15)

🔒 Content Area Liter...	9
🔒 ELTL 500	35
🔒 ELTL 504	40
🔒 ELTL 625	8
ERDG 504	16
ERDG 655	12
🔒 Fun!	3
🔒 Literacy Coaching	25
🔒 OER	5

Blogstitute 2017: Teaching globally to make a difference in the world - The Stenhou   Jul 28, 17
blog.stenhouse.com   teaching   difference   world   blog

ILA 2017 When a Window Becomes a Mirror - Google Slides   Jul 24, 17
docs.google.com

Mindset Kit | Resources for growth and learning mindsets   Jul 20, 17
www.mindsetkit.org

7 Must-Try Summer Projects with Adobe Spark - Class Tech Tips ⌃   Jun 27, 17
classtechtips.com
in outliners: Digital Literacy

Balanced Literacy: Shared Reading - YouTube
www.youtube.com

PLC Series: Public Celebration Conferences | Heinemann   Jun 06, 17
www.heinemann.com

Reading List for Summer in Participatory Citizenship - Literacy & NCTE   Jun 05, 17
blogs.ncte.org

12 Inspiring STEM Books for Girls | Edutopia   May 31, 17
www.edutopia.org

PLC Series: Write-Alouds | Heinemann   May 30, 17
www.heinemann.com

85 Picture Books or Graphic Novels that Support Social Justice Teaching | May 22, 17
pernillesripp.com

Figure 3.25 (top): *A view of my personal Diigo collection*

Figure 3.26 (right): *A view of my personal Symbaloo collection*

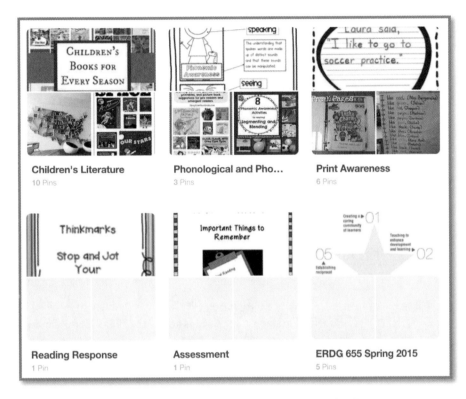

Figure 3.27 (left): *A view of my personal Pinterest boards*

Figure 3.28 (bottom): *A view of my digital citizenship Padlet*

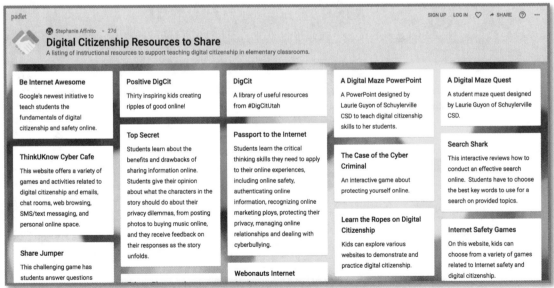

IDEAS FOR CURATED RESOURCE LISTS

Most treasured and accessed sites

Literacy organizations

Favorite children's authors

Sites needed for a unit of study

Collections of sites on a topic (e.g., summer reading, apps for teachers, etc.)

Teacher bloggers to follow

Figure 3.29: *Ideas for curating literacy coaching resources*

Next, choose your content. What tangible piles might you replace with digital ones? What websites do you seem to visit the most and would like to have access to in a single click? Figure 3.29 offers a range of possibilities for curated resource lists.

Shelley Fenton created multiple Symbaloo sites for her teachers, curating the needed and recommended websites as part of her district's writing units of study curriculum. When exploring a new unit of study, Shelley provides all needed links using Symbaloo and posts them on her Google+ Community.

The #cyberPD group uses Padlet to curate artifacts and resources shared from summer book studies. Figure 3.30 shows a shared Padlet wall created for a book study of DIY literacy with teachers across the globe. Here, teachers and coaches shared DIY anchor charts, microprogressions, and bookmarks to visualize how other teachers were creating their own instructional materials for students.

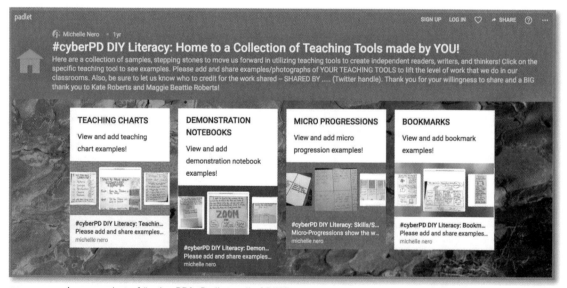

Figure 3.30: *A screenshot of #cyberPD's Padlet wall of DIY literacy resources*

It doesn't matter what tool you choose to compile and curate information, documents, and sites. The goal is to give teachers much needed time to engage with resources rather than search for them.

> **LAUNCHING POINT** ✳
>
> *What information do you wish you had, or wish your teachers had, right at your fingertips? What collection of sites or resources do you wish were all in one place? Well, stop wishing and start curating. First, choose your tool. Next, create a Diigo list, Symbaloo square, or Padlet page to house your materials. Add a few resources to get started and come back over time to continue building it. Most importantly, do not forget to share it with your teachers! Post it on your community page or refer to it in your next professional development session.*

Digitally Create Collaborative Resources

Collaboration, creativity, and curiosity are essential to learning. We need to work together, think together, plan together, and wonder together. By collaborating with our tribe of teachers, we develop our thinking and our toolbox of instructional practices and materials. Collect, curate, and collaboratively create resources with teachers to help them own the learning and the product. I have found that interactive tools and digital bulletin boards, such as Google Docs and Padlet, easily allow for such work.

BE A TECHSPERT

BEGINNING

TECH TOOL

GOOGLE DOCS: *A tool to collaboratively create Web-based documents*

WEBSITE: *www.google.com/docs/about*

COST: *Free!*

TECHSPERT LEVEL: *Great for beginning tech users*

Google Docs provides easy and instant access to shared documents, but it also encourages collaborative creation of them. Together, teachers can compose:

1. Curricular resources: graphic organizers, anchor charts, documents for reading response notebooks, and writing rubrics or checklists

2. Teaching toolkits (Roberts and Beattie Roberts 2016): Anchor charts, demonstration notebook pages, microprogressions, and bookmarks to facilitate student learning and independence

3. Classroom resources: Templates for reading and writing workshop, resources for units of study and shared projects

4. School resources: letters for students and parents, website announcements, and special projects

By curating and creating these documents together, we promote a culture of sharing in the school. Padlet is another good way to curate thinking and resources with others. Together, you and your teachers can share Internet links, files, and pictures with a brief description to invite exploration. Figure 3.31 provides a picture of my "Summer Reading" Padlet, a resource page that promotes summer reading, gathered from teachers and other digital sources.

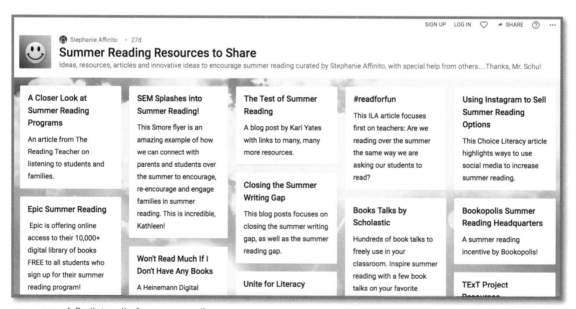

Figure 3.31: *A Padlet wall of summer reading resources*

How might you try this in your work? Start by creating a Padlet wall for each of the grade levels you work with. You might introduce the wall in a grade-level meeting and model how to add a tile. Give teachers time to try it out and double-click on the wall to add a teacher's favorite resource. Encourage teachers to add to their collection over time, building a resource of instructional favorites. You might also create Padlet walls based on specific topics. Choose a topic that teachers have expressed interest in and create a wall to support their efforts. Link to engaging resources, insightful blog posts, instructional resources, and interesting sites. Share it with teachers and encourage them to add to it.

Inspired by Coiro's (2015) work on online inquiry and wonder, a group of teachers chose to explore with their students a common topic, the magic of spring. Each contributed authentic text and multimodal resources that would build on elementary students' curiosities and encourage authentic learning. Together, we compiled instructional resources we might use in our own classrooms—a product of joint effort and inspiration. See Figure 3.32 for the screenshot.

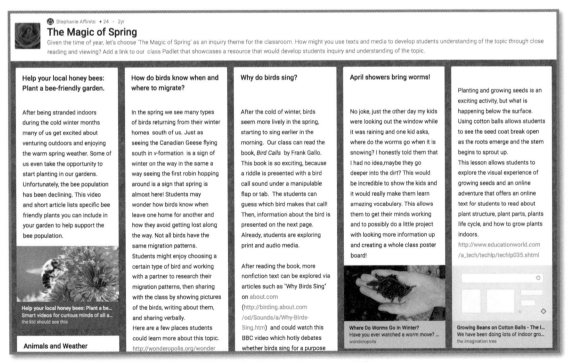

Figure 3.32: *A screenshot of "The Magic of Spring" collaboratively created theme*

As you create opportunities for teachers to work together, they see firsthand the influence that working collaboratively has on their own professional learning and instructional toolkits. Through conversations, common goals, and shared learning, we become better and stronger, often ending up with products that would not be possible if we worked alone. Teachers can then transfer those ideas to their classrooms, providing opportunities for their own students to do the same.

LAUNCHING POINT ✳

With teachers, choose a topic for which they'd like resources. Create a Padlet wall and send it to teachers so they can make contributions. If necessary, send along a short tutorial on Padlet if it is new to them. Thank teachers for their contributions and showcase them at your next professional development session. Link the Padlet to your community page so teachers can access it when they need it the most.

Choose Intentional Coaching Goals

Armed with the information from this chapter, where might you begin? Use the "If-Then-With" chart in Figure 3.33 to help choose an intentional coaching goal for your work ahead. It will easily pair you with a pedagogical focus and a small group of select tools to help you get started.

IF YOU WANT TO . . .	THEN . . .	WITH THESE TOOLS . . .
Redesign your professional development sessions	Digitally differentiate professional development	Google Forms
	Reimagine presentations with multimodal tools	Pixteller, Notography, Tagxedo, Recite
	Promote teacher engagement	Google Forms, Padlet, QR codes, TodaysMeet
Flip literacy coaching for personalized learning	Create guided lessons and tutorials	Screencast-o-Matic, Educreations
	Create interactive documents	ThingLink, QR codes
	Cultivate digital portfolios of teaching and practice	Google Drive, Google+ Communities, Padlet
Provide teachers with needed resources	Curate shared resources	Diigo, Symbaloo, Pinterest
	Create collaborative resources	Google Docs, Padlet

Figure 3.33: *Use the "If-Then-With" chart to choose intentional literacy coaching goals.*

CHAPTER 4

Collaborate with Teachers to Impact Student Learning

I began my literacy coaching career when coaching was brand-new. Back then, if you were to ask what a literacy coach was and what a literacy coach did, you would get a funny look, a slight head tilt, and a different response from each person you asked. Over time and with practice, I came to refine my own personal definition of what literacy coaching was, but I was struck by how different each of our roles really is across schools and educational settings. I was so intrigued by these differences that I spent several years researching exactly what literacy coaches did and why they did it, as part of my doctoral dissertation. I discovered that literacy coaching was different depending on the school, district, or policies in place in each school (Affinito 2011). Regardless of these differences in coaching roles, coaches believed that their primary responsibility was to support teachers and their students, a role they believed was best done in actual classrooms. Literacy coaches observe student engagement and response to instruction, collaborate to teach lessons and try new instructional techniques, and ensure that support is varied and relevant for each teacher. By providing this kind of support right within the classroom, we ensure that our work impacts instruction and ultimately, student learning.

Early in my graduate education program, I completed a course on literacy leadership. Throughout the semester, we read widely about literacy instruction and literacy reform, learned about professional development principles for teachers, and examined policies and practices that impacted our schools. My professor and eventual colleague, Dr. Sean Walmsley, said something that has stayed with me throughout my entire career. After spending multiple classes discussing the various factors that impact literacy reform and what we could do as future literacy specialists to advocate for our teachers and students, he said, "But remember. Nothing happens until it happens in the classroom." Simple, yet powerful words. As coaches and literacy professionals, we juggle multiple responsibilities, each holding the potential to impact student learning. Yet, the bottom line is that nothing we do will impact students unless teachers choose to apply their new learning to the classroom. By connecting with teachers in their actual classrooms and with their actual students and by focusing on topics that they actually want and need to work with, we are ensuring that our coaching makes an impact on student learning. Classroom coaching is at the heart of what we do as literacy coaches.

Why It's Important to Collaborate with Teachers to Impact Student Learning

Research shows teachers' knowledge, skills, and instructional practices influence student achievement (Darling-Hammond 2006; Snow, Griffin, and Burns 2005). Ultimately, literacy leadership and coaching rely on the assumption that coaching practices lead to changes in teacher knowledge and practice, which result in positive changes in student performance (Lockwood, McCombs, and Marsh 2010). By partnering together, we view our instruction with new eyes and envision new possibilities to meet students' needs in the classroom.

The Remodeling Literacy Learning report commissioned by the National Center for Literacy Education (NCLE) (2013) emphasized that teacher collaboration was essential to meeting rising literacy expectations and educators' most powerful professional learning experiences come from working with colleagues. Clear messages emerged from NCLE's (2014) findings that hold particular importance for literacy coaches:

* Engage teachers in focused, purposeful collaboration with colleagues about the instructional shifts that can be made to deepen student literacy learning.

* Create a culture of learning to open classroom doors and share teaching practice so that others can learn from both successes and instructional challenges.

* Commit to continuous, collaborative assessment and analysis of student work to inform instruction.

* Develop and document shared plans for deepening student literacy learning across a school year.

* Choose literacy teaching strategies and materials based on learning from collaborative activities with other teachers.

* Build a coherent school-wide literacy experience for students.

Collaboration comes in many forms, shapes, and sizes. It might begin with teachers working together within a school or district to create curriculum or explore a problem of practice. It might begin with a teacher and a coach connecting to analyze assessment data and create a plan of instruction for students. With the help of technology, our collaborative efforts with teachers can be strengthened and transformed, empowering both teachers and coaches to better connect, collaborate, and reflect. Figure 4.1 outlines the possible ways our traditional methods of collaboration and classroom coaching might expand with the use of digital tools.

The best tools to support this kind of powerful collaboration and coaching are the tools that fit each context and purpose. Teachers engaged in collaborative curriculum work might gather

WITHOUT TECHNOLOGY, Coaches and Teachers . . .	WITH TECHNOLOGY, Coaches and Teachers . . .
Create curriculum and lessons during after-school meetings and on curriculum days.	Collaboratively create curriculum and lessons anytime and anywhere using interactive documents.
Discuss student learning in data meetings.	Document and analyze student learning using digital tools and portfolios.
Create coaching goals and lesson plans through in-person conversations.	Create coaching goals and lesson plans using digital tools for continual reflection and goal setting.
Share coaching plans in hard-copy format for feedback and discussion.	Create and share coaching resources as part of a digital coaching toolkit.
Engage in coaching conversations through in-person meetings.	Reflect digitally on coaching sessions and respond to ideas and feedback.

Figure 4.1: *Literacy coaching activities with and without technology*

the standards, current curriculum documents, chart paper and markers, sticky notes, and other personal note-taking tools. Teachers collaborating about students might utilize assessment data, professional texts, and input from other faculty. The tools of collaboration depend on our teachers, our inquiries, and our available resources. Over time, these tools have evolved to include more digital possibilities, enhancing partnerships in new ways. In addition to in-person discussions and traditional tools, teachers might use the Internet to access supplemental resources or useful websites; look up helpful texts, articles, or blogs; search Twitter; consult a Facebook community; or email other professionals. Teachers might replace chart paper with digital bulletin boards walls or create documents through Google Docs for greater collaboration and ownership. Figure 4.2 offers ways to reimagine traditional tools to facilitate collaboration and coaching with technology. Use these tools to connect and partner with teachers and renew enthusiasm for working together in innovative ways.

TRADITIONAL TOOLS of Collaboration	DIGITAL TOOLS of Collaboration
Large pieces of chart paper or sticky notes	Digital bulletin boards
Notebooks and paper for note-taking	Collaborative note-taking through digital documents
Copies of lessons and instructional materials	Shared documents in virtual drives
In-person discussion	Digital and virtual conversation
Printed books, lessons, and teaching artifacts	Digital books, lessons, and teaching artifacts
Spiral-bound coaching journals and notebooks	Digital shared coaching journals and notebooks

Figure 4.2: *Traditional literacy coaching tools and digital transformation*

Create a Culture of Inquiry and Shared Learning

As teachers, we foster wonder and curiosity for learning in our students. We create empowered, engaged learners when we support students to explore topics they are truly interested in. Harvey and Daniels (2009) note that "teachers in classrooms that nurture curiosity create an irresistible urge to wonder" (94). So, why not create that same irresistible urge to wonder together for the teachers we work with? There are some ways you might set the tone of shared learning in your school community:

1. Share your reading and writing lives: Leave the titles of coach and teacher behind and simply engage as readers and writers.

2. Remain a learner: Although coaching requires us to lead the learning of others, be sure to focus on your own continued professional learning and make that process visible for your teachers.

3. Stay connected to classrooms: Spend time in classrooms to observe students, try out new instructional techniques, and stay in touch with the realities of classroom teaching. Teachers respect coaches who are "in the trenches," and the camaraderie that comes from coteaching is powerful.

4. Work collaboratively: Learn and teach side by side with teachers. Build trusting relationships, find positive entry points for each teacher you work with, and lead a community of inquiry and shared decision making.

5. Ground yourself in the work of students: Build your conversations around student work. Notice and name what you see and connect to instructional practices. Keep these conversations positive, generative, and open to multiple perspectives.

6. Advocate for teachers and students: Push for "strong learning communities, continued professional development, collaboration, and a thoughtful examination of literacy practices" (Dozier 2008, 17). Set clear, intentional goals and encourage all voices to be heard in your conversations.

We have the power to transform the culture of learning in our schools. By focusing on building collaborations with teachers, we harness the power of our collective expertise to improve literacy instruction and achievement. These shared experiences build community and pave the way for more intentional collaboration and classroom coaching.

Generate Living Curriculum

Calkins, Ehrenworth, and Lehman (2012) advise teachers to read our learning standards as if they were gold, making a conscious choice as teachers to see hope and opportunity within our curriculum to accelerate student learning. They urge "teaching toward clearer and higher expectations and doing this work in transparent, collegial and accountable ways, with teachers working together within and between grade levels to be sure that students make observable progress along trajectories of skills development" (2012, 15). Together, literacy coaches and teachers develop a common language of instruction, create a vision for learning, and ensure horizontal and vertical alignment of curriculum to make the greatest impact on student learning. Digital tools can support this important work in three productive ways: ensure easy and accurate access to important curriculum documents, encourage collaborative creation of curriculum and sharing of successful lessons, and foster conversations across and within grade levels.

Often, important curriculum documents are hard to find, may be out of date, or each teacher may have a slightly different version of them. This not only causes frustration for teachers but interferes with the effectiveness of our curriculum and teaching. Coaches need to provide easy and public access to the documents important to teaching: standards, curriculum, assessment tools, and more. Although many of us take comfort in hard copies of these documents, we all know that they can easily be misplaced, inadvertently thrown away, or confused with earlier versions of the same printed document. Digital tools can help us house and organize important documents in a safe, central location and provide easy access to the documents teachers need most. When documents are updated, these newer versions can easily be shared with teachers for immediate reference and use, replacing outdated or inaccurate information instantly.

One option is to use Google Drive to store and share your important curriculum documents and instructional materials.

BE A TECHSPERT

BEGINNING

TECH TOOL

GOOGLE DRIVE: *Cloud storage and backup*
WEBSITE: *www.google.com/drive*
COST: *Free!*
TECHSPERT LEVEL: *Great for beginning tech users*

By creating a shared drive for your teachers, you can add literacy documents for easy access, updating when necessary to ensure teachers have the most up-to-date versions of all materials. Our New York literacy coach group utilizes a shared Google Drive where we keep all session materials. Our ideas are curated and materials can be easily shared by the teachers we work with.

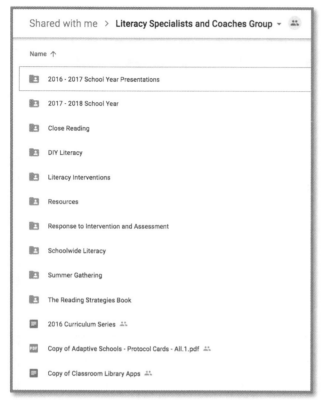

Figure 4.3: *A screenshot of our New York State literacy coach group shared drive*

See Figure 4.3 for a picture of our shared drive. Although I prefer Google Drive, using Dropbox, an alternative drive within the district, or even a private section on the school website, is just as effective.

The best curriculums are those that teachers create while considering the needs of their students, their schools, and the standards. Using a workshop approach, teachers engage their students in authentic reading and writing with strategic, targeted, and explicit minilessons built on the strengths and needs of the students. Although a program or scope and sequence might guide teachers' thinking, no single curriculum will meet the needs of all students in a classroom, in a school, or over time. Instead, the curriculum needs to be generative, changing as the students' knowledge, skills, and dispositions as readers change along with current research on effective literacy instruction.

This kind of curriculum work is best generated by the teachers themselves. By introducing digital tools into our curriculum work with teachers, we can coplan and collaborate synchronously or asynchronously, in person, digitally, or even virtually. These are not scripted documents posted by administration to be followed; they are curriculum maps and lessons created and revised by teachers, giving power to those who know their grade and students the best. On the International Literacy Association's *Literacy Daily* blog, Julie Wise and Meg

Scan the QR code to read Wise and Rishel's blog post on using Google Docs.
http://bit.ly/2ADo8Cn

Rishel (2016) blogged about their experiences creating living curriculum. In their post, they describe their process for creating an online, interactive living curriculum using Google Docs. They believe utilizing Google Docs cultivated a community of collaboration and connection as teachers tended to the living curriculum. Teachers maintained their curriculum writing efforts over time, keeping teaching and learning as alive and ever changing as the documents themselves. Scan the QR code to read their helpful blog post.

When we create and house curriculum digitally, it encourages vertical examination and alignment. Encourage teachers to look beyond their own grade level when planning curriculum, paying careful attention to the scaffolding of standards and instruction within grade-level bands. Teachers can comment on curriculum, ask questions, request clarification, and build a culture of learning and collaboration across grade levels. Ultimately, students benefit.

> **LAUNCHING POINT** ✳
>
> *Complete a little challenge. Right now, try to find the curriculum and assessment documents that teachers need most. Were you able to access them digitally? Are the versions correct and up-to-date? If so, congratulations! If not, create a shared drive or folder and begin updating and housing important literacy documents: standards, curriculum, assessment, and district resources. Your teachers will thank you for compiling these needed documents in one easy-to-access space.*

Interactively Analyze Assessment Data

Literacy coaches have multiple opportunities to document, analyze, reflect on, and celebrate teaching and learning. Many coaches engage in a combination of the following:

✳ Faculty meetings focused on assessment data: Schools are working more closely with assessment data than ever before. As part of response to intervention, schools screen students multiple times per year to ensure progress is being made and to provide supportive tiers of intervention as soon as a gap in performance is noted. Coaches often play a key role in coordinating these assessments, evaluating students and analyzing the data collected.

✳ Grade-level team meetings: Many coaches work in grade-level teams to analyze assessment data specific to teachers' classrooms and grade levels. We might review standardized test results, analyze student writing samples, and collect anecdotal evidence to document the effectiveness of the literacy program and students' growth across the school year.

* Literacy data meetings: Many literacy coaches play a pivotal role in literacy data team meetings and response to intervention meetings. Armed with specialized knowledge about literacy, literacy development, and interpreting assessment data, coaches can provide insight into student development and targeted intervention plans.

* Individual sessions with teachers: Much of our coaching work takes place in the classroom, so we can examine student work with an eye toward the teacher's next steps, lessons, or unit of study.

Our coaching practices can help cultivate a positive culture of reflection around student data. Work to broaden teachers' understanding of the scope and purpose of analyzing assessment data. It should not be a chore, but a celebration of learning. Every interaction, observation, and artifact of learning are data we can use to inform our instruction and understanding of student achievement. Figure 4.4 provides a list of artifacts that could inform our instruction and overall curriculum.

In classrooms, we teach students simple routines for how to learn best in the classroom: guidelines for literacy stations, proper behavior during read-alouds, the structures needed for independent reading time, and more. When students have clear expectations and routines, they are able to focus their time and attention on the task at hand. The same thinking also applies to our work with teachers. When teachers have clear expectations and routines for analyzing assessment data, they can focus their time and attention on the task at hand: gaining useful information to inform their literacy instruction and intervention. Although there are many protocols available for examining assessment data with teachers, I follow three simple guidelines for my work with teachers:

TYPES OF ASSESSMENT DATA

Classroom conversations (student–student, teacher–student)

Writing samples

Running records

Literacy station artifacts

Lesson artifacts (graphic organizers, reading logs, worksheets, etc.)

Informal assessments (letter-sound inventories, sight word inventories, spelling inventories)

Formal assessments (reading inventories, computerized measures)

Figure 4.4: *Types of student assessment data for analysis*

* Operate from a lens of strength: Show teachers how to notice what is going well in their teaching and what students know and can do. Often, teachers want to focus on what is wrong, or what is missing, but this does not move the conversation forward in productive ways.

✳ Follow an "I Notice, I Wonder" protocol: Make observations about the data in front of you and think carefully and critically about what it tells us. What other information might be needed? What assumptions do we need to unpack? What perspective are we taking? Whose perspective are we leaving out?

✳ Link problems to solutions: It can be easy to focus on the things we cannot control, but we need to shift that mind-set to one of action and train ourselves to immediately follow up negative thinking with positive possibilities. Our students deserve nothing less.

Above all, celebrate teaching and learning. Cultivate a culture where student data are celebrated and mined for signs of learning. Technology and digital tools provide new opportunities to do just that. In one upstate New York district, Kristen Abrams, a literacy specialist in a K–5 building, uses Google Drive to lead her literacy data meetings. All important documents and assessment data are housed in Google Drive, accessible only by school faculty. During data meetings, Kristen displays benchmark and individual assessment data for teachers to readily analyze and discuss. This district also uses Google Docs to collaboratively create Response to Intervention plans and progress reports on individual students. This allows teachers to instantly access needed instructional and assessment information on their students across intervention providers. Although screenshots of her Google Drive cannot be shared to protect teacher and student privacy, Figure 4.5 offers a hypothetical look at what her Google Drive folders look like.

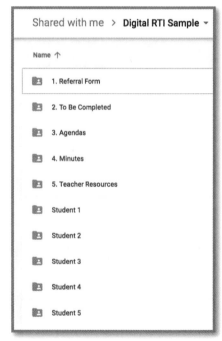

Figure 4.5: *A screenshot of a hypothetical Google Drive to support Response to Intervention*

Digital portfolios can also document student learning and provide another method for analyzing student assessment data. As a coach, you can model what this might look like for a particular student. Build an authentic portfolio of a student's performance comprising multiple pieces of data, using a tool such as Seesaw Learning Journal. Seesaw Learning Journal is a digital portfolio tool that captures student learning and records student progress.

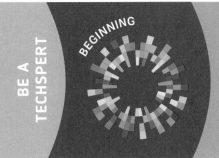

TECH TOOL

SEESAW LEARNING JOURNAL: *A digital portfolio*
WEBSITE: *https://web.seesaw.me*
COST: *Free! Premium plans vary.*
TECHSPERT LEVEL: *Great for beginning tech users*

Take pictures of formal assessment results, include snapshots of classroom interactions, and videotape participation within the classroom. Figure 4.6 provides screenshots of pages from an elementary student's journal captured through Seesaw Learning Journal.

Use these digital portfolios to discuss student performance with others and keep conversations focused on student data. This work can then easily be shared with other teachers the student works with, fostering coherence and coordination of instruction. These portfolios can also be shared with the student's parents or guardians. By using a tool like this in our coaching, we are modeling authentic assessment and conversations grounded in student data. Teachers

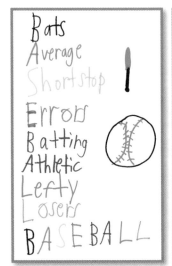

Figure 4.6: *Pages from an elementary student's Seesaw Learning Journal*

will apply these same ideas to their own classrooms, using digital portfolios to encourage deeper learning and reflection and create a strong connection with parents.

> **LAUNCHING POINT** ✳
>
> *Take stock of your current Response to Intervention practices and identify a place where digital documents might streamline the process for teachers. Start by digitizing one document and share it with your administration and colleagues for feedback. Together, brainstorm how digital tools could support your work as a team.*

Partner for Intentional Classroom Coaching

All aspects of literacy coaching have the potential to impact the classroom and student learning, but coaching in the classroom places the focus squarely on the teachers and students. Coaching in the classroom can come in many forms depending on the individual teacher and their students. Dozier (2006) reminds us change occurs "at different times, in different ways, for different people" (141) so coaching must be flexible to meet the individual needs of teachers and the changing nature of those needs over time and practice. As a coach, there are multiple things we can do to ensure our coaching in the classroom is a positive learning experience for both teacher and coach:

* ✳ Be a good listener. Really listen to what teachers say they want and need in the classroom. Be sure that their voices are heard.

* ✳ Follow the teacher's lead. Although you may have ideas for your classroom coaching, follow the teacher's lead and start there. Your initial ideas can come later in the coaching process when the teacher is ready for them.

* ✳ Be trustworthy. Maintain the teacher's confidentiality at all times. I jokingly tell the teachers I work with that our coaching space is like Vegas: What happens in Vegas, stays in Vegas. Teachers need to know they can trust you.

* ✳ Seek out strengths. Find positives in any situation and build on them. Just as we encourage teachers to avoid taking a deficit view when looking at student data, we should have them do the same for themselves. Focus on what is right first and then choose goals together.

✳ Celebrate growth. Big changes in instruction do not happen overnight. Celebrate the small steps of growth you see in the classroom and view them as momentum for larger changes ahead. Every journey starts with one step forward.

Creating this underlying feeling of trust and building caring relationships with teachers is essential to our work and leads to more intensive coaching relationships. Digital tools can support our work in all stages of classroom coaching: invite teachers to collaborate, create a vision for coaching, develop a coaching toolkit, and reflect on teaching and learning.

Invite Teachers to Collaborate

Before we can coach in the classroom alongside teachers, we must first be invited into it. Literacy coaches understand just how difficult this can sometimes be. Teachers must not only feel comfortable with you as a coach, they must feel comfortable with themselves as a teacher to invite reflection and innovation to their instruction. They must feel trusted and supported and understand that coaching is nonevaluative. They must want to invite you into their classrooms, not be forced to, and truly understand the power of working together. Therefore, we must invite teachers into a coaching partnership. Although these invitations can certainly be extended in person through old-fashioned conversation, digital tools offer new ways to spark teachers' interest, pique their curiosity, and encourage them to say "Yes!" to working with you. Here are some things that literacy coaches have tried:

✳ The mass email to school faculty: You know this email. It's the one that you send every year at the same time, inviting teachers to work with you. It might be the "back-to-school kickoff" email, the "new instructional resolutions" email, or the simple "remember I am here to help" email. You send a friendly invitation to all school faculty members with a few ideas of what you might accomplish together and hope for some takers.

✳ The personal email to individual teachers: This email is a bit more personal than the first example and specifically invites individual teachers to collaborate. You might start with teachers you know are always up for working together. Another approach is to share a new resource with a resistant teacher and offer support in trying it in the classroom. This approach usually garners more attention. If you provide teachers with something immediately helpful and applicable to their classrooms, they are more willing to engage with you.

✳ The personally designed digital invitation: Although sending an email gets the job done, personalized digital invitations are much more appealing. Opening a beautiful digital invitation addressed to the whole faculty or customized for each teacher promotes a feeling of professionalism and quite simply is more tempting to open and read. Kristin Houser, a literacy coach in Colorado, recommends using Evite as a way to begin, but you might also explore using Punchbowl, Smilebox, Zazzle, or even Smore. See Figure 4.7 for an example.

✳ The video invitation: With so many digital tools available to create videos, with some on our smartphones, it is easier than ever to personally connect with teachers with a coaching invitation. Imagine how intrigued teachers will be if you sent them a personal video invitation for coaching? If you take the time to personally invite teachers in an innovative way, teachers may give you the same time and investment in return.

Inviting someone into your classroom can feel unsettling for many teachers. By going the extra mile and inviting teachers to collaborate with you, you are setting a positive tone for learning together. This starts with the invitation, but ends with the thank-you! Don't forget to put as much care and attention into thanking teachers for the privilege to work with them. In your thank-you note, make sure to include something positive about the teacher's instruction, the students' work, or the classroom environment.

Figure 4.7: *A personal invitation to engage in literacy coaching*

LAUNCHING POINT *
You might be surprised at how far a little beautification of our coaching can go. Create a personalized digital invitation for coaching using Evite, Smilebox, or Zazzle. Have some fun and play around with the different designs, fonts, and features. Share your invitation with your teachers and see what happens.

Craft a Vision for Coaching

Literacy coaches provide a collegial and nonevaluative atmosphere for coaching. As such, we need to approach classroom coaching as a collaborative endeavor in pursuit of a shared goal to learn together for the sake of students. I distinctly remember one of the first times I provided a demonstration lesson as a new literacy coach. I prepared diligently, but things just did not go as planned. The materials were cumbersome, the students did not have the background knowledge I assumed they had, and on and on. As soon as the lesson was over, the teacher looked at me with a sly smile and said, "Well that did not go as planned, did it?" In that moment I realized my mistake. I came into the classroom with preconceived notions of what the students and teacher needed. I planned and prepared a lesson in isolation. I did not share my plans with the teacher, did not invite collaboration and feedback. Instead, I walked in ready to go, implying that only my perspective mattered.

Now, when I work with teachers in the classroom, the partnership starts immediately. Together, create a vision for your collaboration that includes the following:

* Goal: Identify the focus of your work together. Is it to strengthen reading minilessons? To improve conferencing skills? Name the goal of coaching and discuss the knowledge and resources needed to support such work.

* Process: Next, choose your coaching method based on your goal. Which kind of classroom coaching is best? A series of demonstration lessons? Mindful coteaching? Classroom observations to first identify teacher and student strengths? Or

perhaps a combination will best suit your needs. Clearly articulate the kind of work you will do together in the classroom and discuss each of your roles and responsibilities. Classroom coaching does not provide an opportunity for teachers to grade papers or run to the copier while you demonstrate a lesson to the class. Ensure that the purpose and expectations are clear.

* Logistics: Coaching is all in the logistics. Schedule time to not only work together in the classroom, but for any other groundwork needed for the lesson and to debrief and reflect after the lesson. Is classroom coverage needed? Be sure to take care of those details as well.

It is very important that documentation of your classroom coaching be transparent. Each of the elements previously mentioned must be planned for, noted, and shared. There are no secret agendas, no secret notes, and no secret conversations about your collaborations with teachers. Coaching is purely nonevaluative and therefore should be a shared endeavor from the start. Technology can enhance this transparency, facilitate collaboration, and archive your coaching through shared drives, folders, and documents.

A blank Google Doc is all that you need to start a record of your coaching partnership and create a vision for coaching together. Simply take notes on the goals, process, and logistics for your partnership and go from there. But if you yearn for more structure and organization to streamline the process, as I do, you might create a simple template to guide your work. See Figure 4.8 for a coaching vision plan template and example of what a completed one might look like.

LAUNCHING POINT ✳

What templates do you use to guide your planning and coaching conversations? Think about how you might create digital, shared versions of these documents with your teachers. Download the templates provided or create your own and try using them in your next coaching cycle.

Literacy Coaching Vision Plan

Coaching Partnership: Stephanie and Logan, 2nd grade

GOAL: *What is your instructional focus?*	Add greater student interaction to read-alouds to deepen vocabulary and strengthen higher-level thinking using the Book–Head–Heart framework.	
PROCESS: *What kind of coaching will best meet your goal?* • *Demonstration?* • *Coteaching?* • *Observation?* • *Combination?*	*What will the teacher do?* Observe for: • How I invite students into conversation • How students respond to BHH framework • Which students might need additional support	*What will the coach do?* • Create and share the lesson plan • Demonstrate an interactive read-aloud lesson • Create anchor chart with students
	What resources are needed? • Read-aloud: Excerpt of current book reading in class: *Raymie Nightengale* • Chart paper and markers	
LOGISTICS: *What time and tasks are needed to be successful?*	*Precoaching conversation:* Digital discussion of lesson plan through Google Docs	
	Classroom coaching: Tuesday at 8:40am	
	Postcoaching conversation: Tuesday planning period at 10:25am	
	Classroom coverage? None needed	

APPENDIX A —— Literacy Coaching Vision Plan

Coaching Partnership: _____

GOAL: *What is your instructional focus?*		
PROCESS: *What kind of coaching will best meet your goal?* • *Demonstration?* • *Coteaching?* • *Observation?* • *Combination?*	*What will the teacher do?*	*What will the coach do?*
	What resources are needed?	
LOGISTICS: *What time and tasks are needed to be successful?*	*Precoaching conversation:*	
	Classroom coaching:	
	Postcoaching conversation:	
	Classroom coverage?	

NOTES, OBSERVATIONS, AND QUESTIONS:

...ESTIONS:

Figure 4.8: *A template for a coaching vision plan with an example using an interactive read-aloud lesson*

Create Coaching Plans

Once you have formulated your vision for coaching, you need to decide on the most appropriate coaching practices to support your work and create a plan for your time in the classroom. There are no rules and no single right way to coach in the classroom, but typically, coaches engage in four types of practices in the classroom: demonstration lessons, coteaching or copractice lessons, classroom observations, or a combination of all three.

DEMONSTRATION LESSONS

During demonstration lessons, classroom teachers observe the literacy coach teaching a lesson. The focus of the lesson is chosen collaboratively and created based on the teachers' professional goals and/or school curriculum, but the coach leads the teaching in the classroom. Coaches demonstrate concepts, content, skills, or strategies for teachers who are new to a particular kind of instruction or want to refine their use of it through observation, reflection, and conversation. The teacher observes the coach and takes notes on both the teaching and students' performance. After the lesson, the coach and teachers debrief together to discuss their observations, learning, and wonderings.

Back when the idea of close reading was new for many teachers, I demonstrated lessons in multiple classrooms to show teachers exactly what close reading looked like, sounded like, and felt like. I carefully chose a short, powerful text for students to read and discuss and walked them through the various actions of close readers: rereading, sharing thinking, purposefully annotating the text, and discussing thoughts and opinions. I provided the teachers with my lesson plan and added questions for the teacher to consider as she was observing. My goal was to demonstrate a specific way of reading with students and help teachers imagine the possibilities for their own classrooms. Although there are many possibilities for demonstration lessons, your time is limited so you'll want to identify the lessons that will yield the best results. In your work with each teacher, help solve a problem the teacher encounters over and over again, or support his individual teaching goals. Some of my most frequent demonstration lessons that have the most long-term impact for teachers include:

* literacy routines for reading and writing workshop

* whole-group teaching of select standards

* differentiated small-group teaching of skills and strategies

* individual reading and writing conferences with students

* use of specific texts, resources, and/or materials related to curriculum.

APPENDIX B — Demonstration Lesson Plan

Coaching Partnership: _____

Lesson Date: _____

GOAL: *What is your instructional focus?*	
STUDENTS: • *Grade* • *Background* • *Curriculum* • *Rules and routines*	
LESSON: • *Introduction* • *Explicit teaching* • *Guided teaching* • *Independent practice*	
MATERIALS AND RESOURCES: • *Books?* • *Charts and markers?* • *Student materials?*	
THINGS TO THINK ABOUT: • *What else do we need to consider?* • *What artifacts of learning might we reflect on?*	

May be photocopied for classroom use. © 2018 by Stephanie Affinito from Literacy Coaching. Portsmouth, NH: Heinemann.

Figure 4.9: *A template for a demonstration lesson*

Digital templates can support your lesson planning with teachers. I use a very general lesson-planning template for my coaching demonstrations with teachers. This way, I can personalize it based on our purpose and vision for coaching. See Figure 4.9 for an example.

You might also create templates based on the different kinds of demonstration lessons you provide: whole-group instruction, small guided reading groups, literacy stations, and independent reading conferences.

Not all demonstrations have to be done live, in person, in the classroom. Teachers can observe recordings of your lessons completed in other classrooms or can even view lessons from professional organizations and websites. The purpose of the demonstration lesson is to help teachers envision and imagine a new instructional practice or technique in their own classrooms. Both live and recorded lessons can accomplish this purpose. Figure 4.10 provides a listing of resources to find recorded demonstration lessons to share with teachers.

DEMONSTRATION LESSON RESOURCES

Heinemann Digital Library	www.heinemann.com/PD/digitallibrary/
Teachers College Reading and Writing Project	http://readingandwritingproject.org
The Teaching Channel	www.teachingchannel.org
Choice Literacy	www.choiceliteracy.com
Lead Literacy	https://leadliteracy.com

Figure 4.10: *Resources for videotaped demonstration lessons*

COTEACHING LESSONS

In coteaching lessons, coaches and teachers partner to collaboratively try new instructional techniques in the classroom. They learn from each other and work together to lift the level of their instruction. Together, they decide on a shared goal for the classroom, create a plan of action, and reflect on instruction and student performance. I have a special place in my heart for students who experience difficulty with reading and writing; I work with teachers to strengthen and, oftentimes, reimagine instruction for these students. In one coteaching lesson, I collaboratively planned and taught a guided reading group with a first-grade teacher. We met before the lesson to share ideas and plan. We also discussed the dynamics of the particular group of students. During the guided reading lesson, the classroom teacher taught the elements she was most comfortable with and I

Figure 4.11: *A template for coteaching lessons*

taught the elements that were new to her—strategic word work. We shared the teaching and note-taking and met after the lesson to discuss how the students responded and to plan future work together. In other coteaching lessons, teachers and coaches might come together to:

✳ Try innovative instructional techniques.

✳ Learn from each other's teaching strengths.

✳ Team-teach a new unit of study.

✳ Maximize conferring time for student readers and writers.

✳ Try new routines for the classroom, such as literacy stations or Daily 5.

✳ Develop teaching and observation techniques.

✳ Develop shared language for instruction.

The coach and teacher share the lesson planning, teaching, assessment, and reflection throughout the collaboration. Together, they observe students, provide feedback on instruction, and learn in ways not possible without each other. You might find the template in Figure 4.11 helpful to guide your planning.

OBSERVATIONS

Effective literacy coaching is built on our ability to listen and observe teaching. When we observe, we learn more about the teachers and students. We take an inquiry stance to learn more about instruction in the classroom and identify potential areas for collaboration with teachers. In observation lessons, literacy coaches observe classroom instruction with the sole purpose of strengthening instruction and students' response to instruction. The word *observation* tends to conjure images of formal evaluations by administrators, but this is not the case. Instead, coaches act as a second pair of eyes in the room, noticing and naming instructional techniques, observing student behavior and performance, and taking careful notes for later reflection.

I use a simple template to guide my observations of instruction within classrooms. Having more than a few important "look-fors" makes it impossible for me to focus on the overall flow and feel of a lesson and impedes my ability to observe and listen with intention. Instead, I focus on four broad areas: the classroom environment, student engagement, literacy instruction, and literacy content. I take brief notes on what I notice and wonder about to guide our coaching conversation after the visit. A sample of the template I use is provided in Figure 4.12.

In one school, I partnered with a first-grade teacher who wanted to better manage her workshop classroom. I spent an hour or so observing her students during the literacy block and took digital notes. Following the observation, I met with the teacher to debrief and plan future coaching sessions. I returned to my notes and used my

APPENDIX D — Literacy Coaching Observation Notes

Classroom Environment		
LOOK FOR: • Routines • Groupings • Culture of reading • Access to text • Materials and resources	I notice:	I wonder:
Student Engagement		
LOOK FOR: • Active engagement • Varied methods • Teaching tools available? • Balance of teacher/student talk	I notice:	I wonder:
Literacy Instruction		
LOOK FOR: • Balanced literacy framework • Responsive instruction • Differentiation • Teacher language • Pacing • Materials • Assessment	I notice:	I wonder:
Literacy Content		
LOOK FOR: • Skills taught and reinforced • Strategies taught and reinforced • Alignment of instructional language • Appropriate text levels	I notice:	I wonder:

Figure 4.12: *A template for coaching observations*

"I Wonder" statements and questions to start the conversation. We discussed classroom management strategies and transition techniques that might help organize students' independent work time and created a plan of action.

Teachers might also observe each other's classrooms with you as you highlight innovative and effective literacy practices across your school: effective transition techniques, powerful minilessons, or strong reading and writing conferences. When we shift our perceptions of observations from one of evaluation to one of collegial learning, we shift the entire landscape for learning together.

Not all observations have to happen live, in the classroom. Video tools are a powerful way to provide feedback on classroom practices. Teachers can record their own instruction for later viewing and reflection; they can even share those recordings with you for feedback. In the latter scenario, teachers can upload their videos to a private platform, such as Acclaim, a digital tool that allows teachers to easily record, upload, and privately collaborate on their teaching practices with you through video.

BE A TECHSPERT

INTERMEDIATE

TECH TOOL

ACCLAIM: *A platform to create, annotate, and share videos*
WEBSITE: *www.getacclaim.com*
COST: *Premium plans vary.*
TECHSPERT LEVEL: *Good for users with some tech knowledge*

Acclaim gives teachers more control over what they share with you, which reduces anxiety from having someone observe their teaching. Through this video collaboration, you can view teachers' instruction and comment on specific areas she has requested feedback on. Virtual literacy coaching connects teachers and coaches in new ways, fostering professional connections, shared learning, and greater reflection on teaching practice.

COMBINATION OF PRACTICES

Rarely does our work as literacy coaches fit into neat little categories. Instead, coaching is messy and often blurs the lines of what literature says we might do. Your work might be a blend of demonstration lessons, coteaching and copractice lessons, and classroom observations. For example, you might start by demonstrating a minilesson with the whole class. Next, you and the teacher coteach small guided reading groups together. Your visit then ends with the teacher observing your conferences with a few readers. In this example, multiple forms of classroom coaching were used to best meet your shared goals.

Coaching is a shared process of collaboration. As coaches, we may have specialized knowledge about literacy and literacy instruction, but your teachers have specialized knowledge and unique insights about the students in their classrooms. We must fuse our expertise to think in powerful ways about instruction.

Once your coaching vision plan and lesson are complete, share them with your teachers as models for lesson planning, collaboration, and reflection. These documents are important coaching tools and, over time, teachers acquire multiple models for instruction. Ask teachers for their feedback. Use the commenting tool to pose questions at certain points in the lesson or to encourage reflection. These comments not only invite collaboration, they model what we want to teachers to think about and reflect upon. Although your comments should be specific to each teacher and each lesson, here are a few general questions to encourage shared reflection:

* Do you think I provided enough scaffolding here in this book introduction?"

* "This is a level M book. How do you think your students will handle the text features?"

* "I have decided to use an anchor chart to illustrate this concept. What do you think of this sample?"

* "Have you already worked with this mentor text before? It works well to illustrate this writing skill."

* "Let's plan to use your revision checklist. Do you have one or should I bring an example?"

By asking genuine questions about the classroom and the students within it, we are coming from a place of inquiry, not evaluation. We are cultivating a spirit of shared and continual learning, reminding teachers we are partners in literacy instruction. Figure 4.13 provides a screenshot of a collaboratively created intervention lesson with specific comments and personalized feedback.

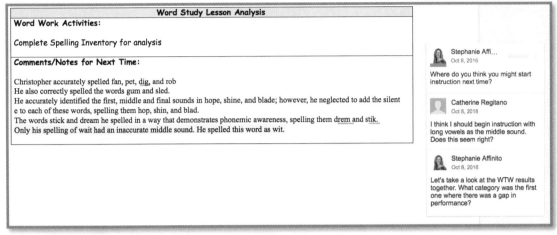

Figure 4.13: *An example of a planned literacy intervention lesson with coaching comments*

> **LAUNCHING POINT**
> ✳
>
> *Head to Google Drive or a private drive on your school's website and create shared folders for each of the teachers you work with. Starting with your next classroom coaching cycle, begin to use one digital document or lesson.*

Create a Digital Coaching Toolkit

During coaching conversations, I often find myself providing on-the-spot demonstrations. I might engage teachers in a brief lesson on phonemic awareness and ask them to sort sounds. I might walk teachers through word-building activities so they experience a new way of engaging students. I might introduce books to teachers to model how they might do the same for their students. I might even create game boards on sticky notes as visuals for teachers to support instructional planning. These demonstrations and notes act as instant and tangible tools to further teacher learning.

Kate and Maggie Roberts (2016) encourage teachers to create teaching tools to support student learning: anchor charts, microprogressions, demonstration notebooks, and bookmarks that provide students with tangible goals and personalized strategies to increase learning and independence. Teachers collect these resources in a toolkit, often a notebook or binder, to use when working with small groups of students or in individual conferences. Logan Fisher, a fourth-grade teacher and literacy coach, uses her toolkit for both reading and writing conferences with students. A picture of her toolkit can be found in Figure 4.14.

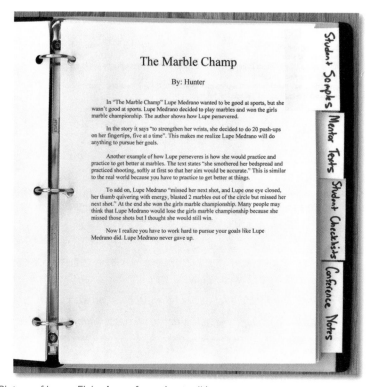

Figure 4.14: *Picture of Logan Fisher's conferencing toolkit*

We can provide the same kinds of supports for our teachers by creating coaching toolkits: a collection of resources to support teacher learning. For example, if you plan to model a small-group lesson on making words, your coaching toolkit might include a picture of the anchor chart created with students, a list of words appropriate to the alphabetic feature students are working on, a game template that can be used for further practice, and a list of helpful reminders for the teacher. Essentially, a coaching toolkit provides you with what you need to support teacher learning and application to the classroom. Your coaching tool kit might include:

❋ anchor charts created in demonstration and coteaching lessons

❋ demonstrations of instructional practices and routines

❋ mentor texts used in literacy lessons

* words lists for early skills teaching

* sample games and graphic organizers to support a lesson

* pictures of literacy classrooms

* student data for reflection and analysis.

A few pages from my coaching toolkit to support teachers' learning about literacy intervention can be found in Figure 4.15.

By creating a digital coaching toolkit, we can share our resources and provide access to them when teachers need them most—when they are planning their next lesson or teaching in the classroom. How? By taking pictures of your physical toolkit and uploading helpful resources and files in a shared space that teachers can access. Google Drive and Padlet are excellent choices for creating digital coaching toolkits. If using Google, create a shared drive that all of your teachers can access. You might create folders for each area of your coaching: read-alouds, minilessons, conferencing, word work, assessment, and so on. Or, you might organize them by content area instead: for example, phonemic awareness, alphabetics, fluency, strategies, comprehension. Choose the organizational method that best fits your coaching. Upload pictures and copies of the items already in your coaching toolkit. Padlet can also be used to create digital coaching toolkits.

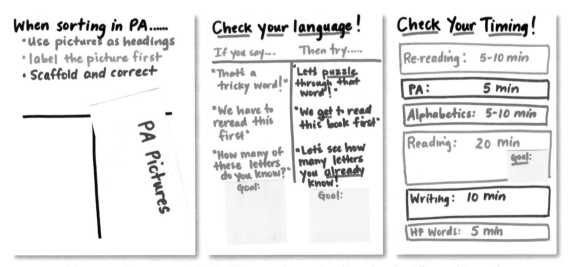

Figure 4.15: *A few pages from my coaching toolkit supporting teachers' learning about literacy intervention*

Create multiple Padlet shelves or walls for each area of your coaching, as Logan did. Figure 4.16 provides a screenshot of her "Up the Ladder" toolkit for her students using Padlet.

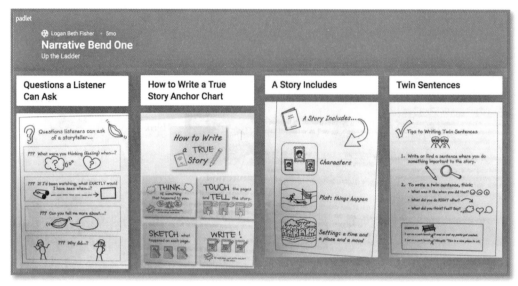

Figure 4.16: *Logan Fisher's "Up the Ladder" coaching toolkit using Padlet*

I created a digital coaching toolkit using Padlet and assigned individual Padlet shelves to each area of my coaching. Figure 4.17 provides a screenshot of my coaching toolkit.

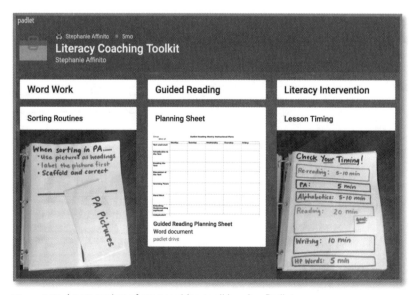

Figure 4.17: *A screenshot of my coaching toolkit using Padlet*

Coaching toolkits provide resources and instructional materials for teachers to access when they need them most, extending your coaching beyond a bounded lesson and enhancing teacher learning.

Reflect on Classroom Coaching

Ideally, following your coaching in the classroom, you can meet with teachers to reflect on the classroom experience, give each other feedback, and pose questions for continued inquiry. If you are fortunate enough to reflect in person, you might use a digital document to capture your conversations and next steps. See Figure 4.18 for an example.

But in a time-crunched world where planning time is precious, this may not be possible. Technology and digital tools can foster these coaching conversations in a digital space. Consider creating a shared document for ideas, thoughts, and reflections from your coaching sessions with a specific teacher. In it, you might plant seed ideas for future coaching partnerships and reflect on coaching experiences.

The easiest way to begin is to return to the coaching vision document and lesson plans referenced early in this chapter. By revising these shared documents together, you send the message that your work is constantly changing and growing. Your goal is to create strong instructional partnerships to benefit students. Revisit the goals, processes, and logistics you envisioned and reflect on how they worked. What might work better next time? Add a new section for joint notes, observations, and questions based on your classroom coaching session. Capture your own thoughts and reflections and ask specific questions to push your teacher's thinking forward. After demonstrating an interactive read-aloud in a kindergarten classroom, I posed this question for the teacher to consider as we planned for a future lesson:

APPENDIX E — Literacy Coaching Conversation

Coaching Partnership: ______	
CELEBRATIONS: *What went well?*	
INQUIRY: • *What did we wonder about?* • *What do we need to consider?* • *What did not feel quite right?*	
STUDENT RESPONSES AND ARTIFACTS OF LEARNING: • *How did students respond?* • *How do we know?* • *What additional supports are needed?*	
NEXT STEPS: • *Revise goals, process, and logistics.* • *What did we learn about literacy teaching?* • *Where could we head next?* • *What do we need?*	

Figure 4.18: *A template for a literacy coaching conversation*

"I think the students responded well to the book we chose! Even though it was a fairly simple text, the quick video introduction and using the map in the classroom made the content come to life. However, I think we had too many stopping points during the read-aloud. We originally thought they would help the students connect to this nonfiction text, but I think it may have distracted them. I think we should plan for fewer stopping points in our next book. What do you think?"

You might rely on a few questions to generate conversation and discussion:

* "What you think about the lesson? What went well? What didn't seem quite right?"

* "How do you feel the students responded? What evidence do we have for their learning?"

* "What do we need to do next to further student learning? What are they ready to know next? What lessons, materials, professional development, and coaching might we plan for?"

* "What did we learn about literacy teaching from our partnership?"

By involving teachers in every step of the coaching cycle, we empower them to feel in control of their own learning. As we complete one coaching cycle, we create new goals that move us forward. Choosing goals is essential to the learning process. For teachers, having a goal does not mean we have problems in our practices; it means we have a vision for moving forward. By choosing new goals with teachers, we put them in charge of their own learning. By documenting those goals, we provide clear and concrete reminders for the journey ahead, and by revisiting these goals, we celebrate the changes we make and model that learning is never complete.

Once a new goal has been set together, it is important to craft opportunities for its realization. It can be easy to state what we will do next and try next, but it is harder to hold ourselves accountable to do so in our busy days as educators. When you create your continued goals, be sure to provide concrete ways for teachers to continue their learning. Make the learning goal visible, name the next time teachers will have a go at the new instructional strategy, follow up with teachers, and offer continued support. It does no good to spend all that time and energy to invite teachers to partner with you, plan mindful and intentional coaching lessons, and reflect on the experience, if it ends there. Learning is not bound into individual, discrete coaching cycles, but is continuous. Be sure to follow up with each teacher a week later, two weeks later, a month later, and so on. Set reminders for yourself through a digital app or print a monthly calendar to help ensure you follow up with teachers. Make a commitment to their continued learning, and show them you are invested in their work.

> **LAUNCHING POINT** ✳
>
> *Take concrete steps to follow up your classroom coaching with continuous teacher support. Set reminders to follow up with each teacher you work with in your digital calendar. Right now, choose a teacher to follow up with and set a digital reminder to check in.*

Choose Intentional Coaching Goals

Armed with the information from this chapter, where might you begin? Use the "If-Then-With" chart in Figure 4.19 to help choose an intentional coaching goal for your work ahead. It will easily pair you with a pedagogical focus and a small group of select tools to help you get started.

IF YOU WANT TO . . .	THEN . . .	WITH THESE TOOLS . . .
Create a culture of inquiry and shared learning	Generate living curriculum	Google Drive, Google Docs
	Interactively analyze assessment data	Google Docs, Seesaw Learning Journal
Partner for intentional classroom coaching	Invite teachers to collaborate	Evite, Smilebox, Smore
	Craft a vision for coaching	Google Drive, Google Docs
	Create coaching plans	Google Drive, Google Docs
	Create a digital coaching toolkit	Google Drive, Padlet
	Reflect on classroom coaching	Google Drive, Google Docs

Figure 4.19: *Use the "If-Then-With" chart to choose intentional literacy coaching goals.*

Find Inspiration

CHAPTER 5

Every journey needs a little inspiration. Years ago, when I was completing my dissertation, I desperately needed inspiration. I was enjoying the journey, but the task of writing while working with three young children afoot was definitely taxing. I sought the company and advice of others, tried to strike a balance between home life and writing (which did not always work), and looked for inspiration wherever I could find it. One of my dissertation chairs had a wonderful habit of signing her emails to me with a single word: *onward*. Whether she was sending recommendations for revisions, new research to read, or ideas for moving forward, I eagerly looked for that single word on her emails: *onward*. Although she may not have known it, that one word was my hope that I was indeed moving onward, even at times where I felt like I was treading water or was lost in the sheer possibilities of analyzing and discussing my results. *Onward*. That one word conveys hope, progress, forward movement, and growth. As you move onward in your own journey as a literacy coach, adding digital tools to your coaching toolkit, I offer you a few nuggets of advice to sustain your work ahead:

1. Choose your digital coaching tools intentionally and strategically.

2. Create a launching pad for your work.

3. Take care of your digital footprint.

4. Nurture your own learning.

5. Connect with others.

Choose Digital Tools Intentionally and Strategically

Fueled with excitement for the innovations you have seen throughout this book, it might be tempting to try them all. Each one has the potential and possibility to transform teacher learning. Yet, too much of a good thing can actually hinder our work. We easily can become lost in the sheer number of possibilities (and potential technical difficulties) that accompany multiple digital tools.

Guided by your coaching goals, begin by choosing a small number of core digital tools. What aspects of your coaching do you want to enhance? What challenges do you face as a coach that technology could help alleviate? Use the "If-Then-With" charts at the end of each chapter and reflect on your responses. Do you see a pattern in your coaching goals? Based on your reflections, did particular tools come up more than once? If so, start there. The tools you choose should be immediately applicable to your work, useful to multiple aspects of your coaching, and something that matches your teachers' level of technology savviness. For example, if you want to create a digital community for your teachers, you might have read about using Google+ and were intrigued. But, if you know most of your teachers are on Facebook, you might create a private community group there instead. If you were excited by using Educreations to create flipped coaching lessons, but your district already uses ShowMe, a similar tool, then start there instead. Although I may have referred to particular digital tools, there are multiple apps that can accomplish the same task, so give yourself permission to explore, to play, and to discover the possibilities that best fit your wants and needs as a coach and the context of your coaching.

It is important to be flexible in our use of digital tools. Choose apps that can be used in multiple ways to reach your coaching goals and provide intentional models for teachers. Take Padlet, a digital bulletin board, as an example. Throughout the book, you read about how I used Padlet to create a literacy community among teachers, to collaboratively share and create teaching resources, and to increase engagement in professional development sessions. See Figures 5.1, 5.2, and 5.3 as examples.

Figure 5.1: *A Padlet wall designed to build a community of readers and learners*

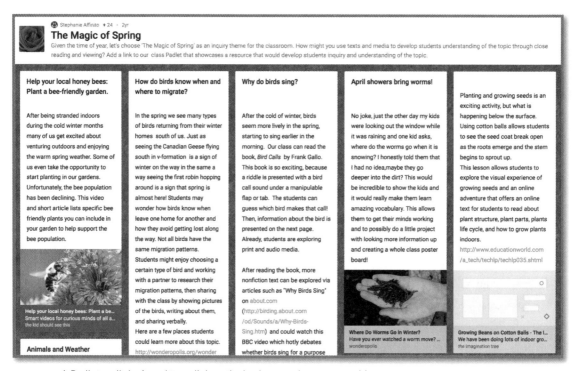

Figure 5.2: *A Padlet wall designed to collaboratively share and create teaching resources*

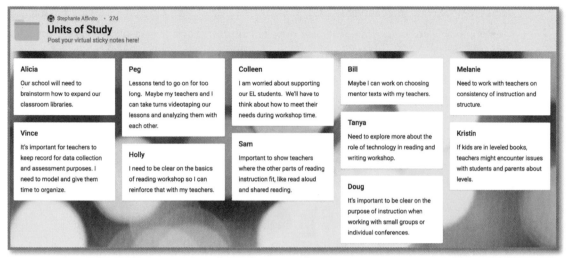

Figure 5.3: *A Padlet wall designed to increase engagement in professional development sessions*

I introduced a single tool to teachers, but demonstrated how to use that tool for different purposes. By cultivating a mind-set for technology, rather than a toolbox of digital tools, we show teachers how to be mindful and strategic decision makers, guided above all by pedagogy.

LAUNCHING POINT ✳

What core digital tools might you use to start your journey into coaching? Go ahead and identify one you could see yourself using with teachers. Then note three different ways that you might use that same tool to demonstrate flexibility to your teachers. Tweet me your favorite core coaching tools to @AffinitoLit!

Create a Launching Pad for Your Work

Organization is critical to our success as literacy coaches. The ways in which we present and organize our coaching spaces matter and the organization of our digital coaching tools and spaces are just as important. As you try the ideas presented through this book, you will find you have multiple new accounts for digital tools and apps to keep track of, exciting new tutorials and interactive documents for teachers to explore saved somewhere on your computer, and new websites and blog posts to share. It can be quite easy to get lost in the sheer volume of information and resources we encounter and create for others. All too often, I find myself searching my Internet history to remember that fantastic new website I stumbled across (but did not save) or need to think carefully about what I named a particular file and where I saved it on my hard drive so I can email it to teachers. I imagine many of you can relate. To make sense of our work and to ensure that the many resources we find and create are easily accessible to our teachers (and to ourselves!), we must have a system for organizing and accessing them easily and quickly. If not, using technology in our coaching will simply become another task or chore to keep track of, rather than intentional and strategic coaching tools with the potential to transform classrooms. I suggest you create a launching pad for your work, a digital coaching space to organize your new coaching tools, and invite teachers to engage with them.

Shelley Fenton uses Google+ for her literacy coaching hub. I've included pictures of various aspects of her hub in Figures 5.4 through 5.9. Although names and faces have been blurred for privacy, you can easily see the format and function of each element within her launching pad.

Just as each literacy coach and coaching position is unique, so too are each coach's launching pads. We can make decisions about the platform we use, the ways we present and share information, and how teachers interact with each other. Here are some specific things about launching pads you might have noticed in Shelley's Google+ example that can serve as guidelines for creating your own:

1. They are easily accessible, depending on your coaching context. Although I use Google Sites, you might choose a more private Google website, Google+ community page, shared Google Drive, or even Google Classroom for the teachers you work with. Ideally, you will choose a platform that integrates with what you already use in your district and makes accessing your launching pad quick and easy for those you work with.

2. They are inviting. Each coach makes conscious decisions about various design elements to welcome and invite teachers to engage with the site. The colors chosen, the pictures used, and the layout of the site are all important. We want this space to be just as inviting as your in-person coaching space so teachers drop by digitally as well.

3. They have spaces for coaching materials and instructional resources. No matter how much time you spend creating digital coaching resources, if teachers cannot

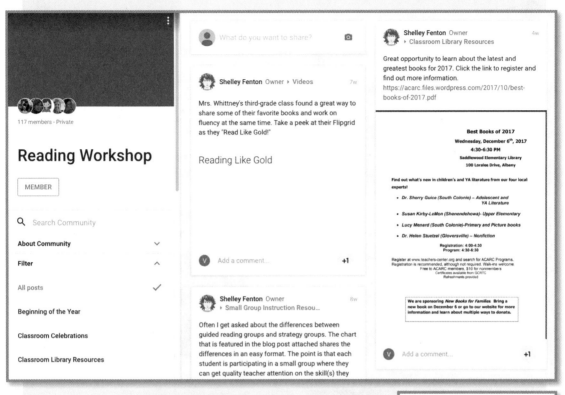

Figure 5.4: *The opening page of Shelley's launching pad*

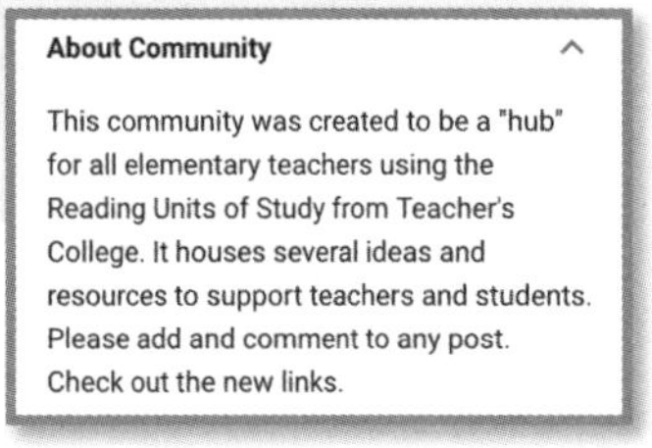

Figure 5.5: *A screenshot of Shelley's discussion categories, which are organized so readers can find information easily*

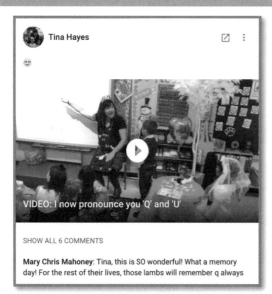

Tina Hayes

VIDEO: I now pronounce you 'Q' and 'U'

SHOW ALL 6 COMMENTS

Mary Chris Mahoney: Tina, this is SO wonderful! What a memory day! For the rest of their lives, those lambs will remember q always

Figure 5.6: *A screenshot of Shelley's post to celebrate instructional innovation and encourage conversation among teachers*

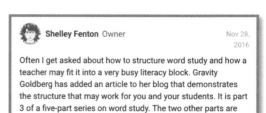

Shelley Fenton Owner   Nov 28, 2016

Often I get asked about how to structure word study and how a teacher may fit it into a very busy literacy block. Gravity Goldberg has added an article to her blog that demonstrates the structure that may work for you and your students. It is part 3 of a five-part series on word study. The two other parts are listed to the right - What is Word Study? and What Do Word Study Notebooks Look Like? It is definitely worth a look!

How might I schedule MY time during word study to meet the needs of all students? |

drgravitygoldberg.com

Figure 5.7: *A screenshot of Shelley's post to share an important blog written by Pam Koutrakos*

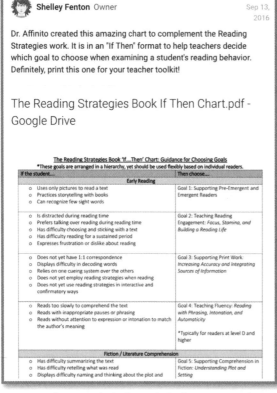

Shelley Fenton Owner   Sep 13, 2016

Dr. Affinito created this amazing chart to complement the Reading Strategies work. It is in an "If Then" format to help teachers decide which goal to choose when examining a student's reading behavior. Definitely, print this one for your teacher toolkit!

The Reading Strategies Book If Then Chart.pdf - Google Drive

Figure 5.8: *A screenshot of a post sharing resources to build our toolbox of teaching ideas*

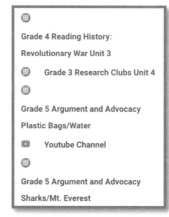

Grade 4 Reading History: Revolutionary War Unit 3

Grade 3 Research Clubs Unit 4

Grade 5 Argument and Advocacy Plastic Bags/Water

Youtube Channel

Grade 5 Argument and Advocacy Sharks/Mt. Everest

Figure 5.9: *Shelley's list of the Symbaloo sites that ease planning for upcoming units of study*

or do not access them, your work is in vain. Your creations cannot be stored on your own personal device where teachers must seek out access. Instead, these materials need to be made available for teachers to view on demand when they need them most. Your launching pad should be an organized space where teachers can easily access your coaching materials and instructional resources. These can be physically placed on your launching pad or linked through Google Drive or Padlet.

4. They celebrate our work as literacy coaches and teachers. Your launching pad is a hub of innovation. It invites teachers to explore and be inspired. Share pictures of effective literacy instruction, link to a video of innovative practices, and highlight the work in your school or district. Notice and name teacher's efforts and celebrate teacher and student learning. Take pictures of teachers working in your professional development sessions, take a selfie with a teacher after an amazing lesson, or capture the beauty of the school as you walk down the student-work-clad hallways.

5. They encourage collaboration. Although a launching pad initiates instructional innovation, it must also sustain it. Just like our curriculum, this hub should be a continual work-in-progress, a living portfolio of coaching, teaching, and learning. Your launching pad should encourage collaboration between and among teachers; it should be a place for a quick hello or a more substantive conversation about classroom instruction. You can include these collaborative features right within your hub or you can link to a Google+ page or even a comment-moderated Padlet wall.

We all need a launching pad, a hub, a command center for our work. As literacy coaches, we can only create instructional change if we connect and collaborate with teachers. Therefore, our coaching materials can only support our work if teachers actually use and interact with them. By ensuring a common, central location to access those coaching tools and inspire teacher learning, we create a place of possibilities.

LAUNCHING POINT ✳

Launching pads, or hubs, are critical to our work. What digital spaces do you have for organizing your coaching life for teachers? If you have one, how might you elevate it to the next level? If you do not yet have one, go ahead and create one!

Take Care of Your Digital Footprint

Teachers have a responsibility to use text, technology, and media critically and strategically for reading, composing, and learning with their students (Muhtaris and Ziemke 2015). We must show students that technology is not just fun and engaging; it helps us partner with others, collaborate to further our learning, and leave a lasting impact on the world for global good. Given its power, we not only have to teach students the tools of technology to enhance their learning, but we also need to teach them how to do so safely and respectfully. Students need to be taught what it means to be a responsible digital citizen. This work begins with our teachers. As coaches, we must model safe, responsible, and effective digital citizenship for teachers, so they can do the same with their students.

Common Sense Education (2015) defines digital citizenship as the ability to think critically, behave safely, and participate responsibly in the digital world. Essentially, digital citizenship is about using technology in safe, respectful, and responsible ways. But beyond that, it is about developing communication, collaboration, critical thinking skills, and creativity (the 4 Cs) to help students harness the power of technology for learning. According to Common Sense Education (2015), there are eight elements of an effective digital citizenship curriculum that should be woven into an integrated digital citizenship curriculum: Internet safety, privacy and security, relationships and communication, cyberbullying and digital drama, digital footprint and reputation, self-image and identity, information literacy, and creative credit and copyright. See Figure 5.10.

It is critical that we also explore digital citizenship with teachers. Although teachers are certainly more savvy about how to act responsibly and respectfully online, digital collaboration and learning might be new for them, as might be the idea of what it means to leave your digital footprint behind each click, swipe, and tap of the keyboard. Here are some guidelines for ways to ensure teachers think carefully about their work with digital tools:

1. Model professional interactions online. Just as we model professional interactions in person through our coaching, we must also model professional interactions in digital and virtual spaces. Always be courteous and respectful, model appropriate postings online, and use a professional, respectful tone at all times.

2. Take care to protect your online persona. I encourage you to google yourself and see what appears. You might be surprised to see more of your personal life displayed online than you would have liked. Check your privacy settings on your

Cross-Curricular Framework

 Privacy & Security

Students learn strategies for managing their online information and keeping it secure from online risks such as identity thieves and phishing. They learn how to create strong passwords, how to avoid scams and schemes, and how to analyze privacy policies.

 Digital Footprint & Reputation

Students learn to protect their own privacy and respect others' privacy. Our digital world is permanent, and with each post, students are building a digital footprint. By encouraging students to self-reflect before they self-reveal, they will consider how what they share online can impact themselves and others.

 Self-Image & Identity

These lessons are designed to help students explore their own digital lives, focusing on their online versus their offline identity. Students learn the benefits and risks of presenting themselves through different personas and the effects on their sense of self, their reputation, and their relationships.

 Creative Credit & Copyright

Living in a "copy/paste" culture, students need to reflect on their responsibilities and rights as creators in the online spaces where they consume, create, and share information. From addressing plagiarism to piracy, students learn about copyright and fair use.

 Relationships & Communication

Students reflect on how they can use intra-personal and interpersonal skills to build and strengthen positive online communication and communities. They delve into the concept of digital citizenship and digital ethics, and they reflect on their online interactions.

 Information Literacy

Information literacy includes the ability to identify, find, evaluate, and use information effectively. From effective search strategies to evaluation techniques, students learn how to evaluate the quality, credibility, and validity of websites, and give proper credit.

 Cyberbullying & Digital Drama

Students learn what to do if they are involved in a cyberbullying situation. They explore the roles people play and how individual actions—both negative and positive—can impact their friends and broader communities. Students are encouraged to take the active role of upstander and build positive, supportive online communities.

 Internet Safety

Students explore how the Internet offers an amazing way to collaborate with others world-wide, while staying safe through employing strategies such as distinguishing between inappropriate contact and positive connections. These foundational skills are just the beginning!

 common sense education™

DIGITAL CITIZENSHIP IN A CONNECTED CULTURE ©2015 COMMON SENSE MEDIA www.commonsense.org

Figure 5.10: *An overview of Common Sense Education's digital citizenship curriculum*

social media accounts and take careful measures to safeguard your accounts and passwords. I recommend that you create professional profiles on social media that are separate from your personal accounts to help protect both aspects of your life.

3. Stay safe online. Just as we teach students the hallmarks of an unsafe website or scam, we must do the same for teachers. Use virus protection software, heed warnings about unsafe sites, and evaluate the credibility of the websites you visit, use, and share with teachers. Give teachers the tools to do the same.

4. Respect copyright laws. This is particularly important as teacher entrepreneurship gains popularity. Learn about copyright laws and abide by them at all times. Cite sources throughout your presentations and give credit where credit is due. To preserve the integrity of our profession, ensure that you are not using or purchasing materials that violate these copyright laws.

5. Follow your school's acceptable use policy. Make sure that your digital actions are in accordance with your school's social media and privacy policies. Do not share student photos or student work online or through social media unless permitted. If your school does not yet have an acceptable use policy, help create one using resources from Edutopia. Scan the QR code to view Edutopia's guidelines.

Scan the QR code to view Edutopia's guidelines for school social media use.
http://edut.to/2kyRrjP

By modeling these behaviors and noticing and naming them with teachers, we ensure they find their way into our classrooms. Figure 5.11 offers a listing of helpful resources on digital citizenship for our work as coaches and in the classroom.

Nurture Your Own Learning

As literacy coaches, we are constantly placing others' learning needs over our own: the teachers and administrators we work with, their students and parents, and even the community. To be effective coaches, we must continue our own learning process, even as we lead the learning of others. We must stretch ourselves to new heights, change our practices based on new ideas and experiences, and imagine new possibilities. Transforming our coaching with digital tools is not

DIGITAL CITIZENSHIP RESOURCES	
Common Sense Media Digital Citizenship	www.commonsensemedia.org/educators/digital-citizenship
International Society for Technology in Education Citizenship in Digital Age	www.iste.org/explore/articleDetail?articleid=192
InCtrl	www.teachinctrl.org
Digizen	www.digizen.org
Educator's Corner	http://iitgbadges.wixsite.com/educatorscorner
Google Be Internet Awesome	https://beinternetawesome.withgoogle.com

Figure 5.11: *Resources to support teaching digital citizenship*

simply about adding technology to our current coaching practices. It is about using technology and digital tools to make our coaching more authentic, meaningful, and effective. Through technology, we better illustrate our coaching content, learn through the company of others, and better connect with teachers. So, continuing our own learning is not about taking a workshop on how to better use Google or how to add Padlet to your coaching toolkit. It is about looking at coaching with a new lens through the help of technology. How can you continue your own journey to grow your own coaching practices?

1. Continue your education and take a class at a local university. Take a class in literacy content to gain new ideas and perspectives, invest in a leadership class to hone your skills, or simply take a class on a topic that interests you.

2. Attend a professional development conference or workshop. Often, we are the ones leading the learning, but attending a conference or workshop as a learner not only provides us with new content to consider but also models new ways of working with our teachers. Take care to note new content and new ways of learning it, and bring these new ideas back to your own sessions.

3. Commit to your reading life. Sometimes, we forget about our own reading lives in pursuit of helping others rediscover theirs. Carve out time for yourself as a reader

of both personal and professional titles. Set personal and professional reading goals and reap the benefits for your coaching.

4. Write and reflect on your coaching practices. As explored in Chapter 2, educational blogging is gaining recognition. Blogging gives us a chance to reflect on our own practice, develop our writing abilities, and connect with others. We reflect on our own philosophies for literacy teaching and learning, hone our craft, and gain inspiration for our continued work. Consider starting your own blog or commit to following those who have.

5. Find a mentor. Meenoo Rami (2014) recommends finding a mentor and Muhtaris and Ziemke (2015) recommend finding an epicenter practitioner. These mentors inspire our work, provide support and resources, and act as guides on the side for those who guide the learning of others. These mentors might be physically close by but can always be a click away digitally. Seek out others to inspire your learning, and remember that you can inspire the learning of others as well. Find a mentor, be a mentor, and watch our profession thrive.

6. Gain inspiration from Podcasts and TED Talks. In our busy schedule, podcasts and inspirational videos can be the perfect spark for learning and continued momentum. Podcasts are episodes of audio files on a variety of topics, even series of shows. Often, these podcasts are brief and are great ways to productively fill your commute to work. Figure 5.12 offers a listing of those that might be of interest.

PODCASTS	
Heinemann podcast library	www.heinemann.com/podcasts.aspx
Reading Rockets podcasts	www.readingrockets.org/podcasts/itunes
Voice of Literacy	www.voiceofliteracy.org
Scholastic book podcasts	www.scholastic.com/bookfairs/books/podcasts
Edutopia podcasts	www.edutopia.org/discussion/podcasts-teachers
International Society for Technology in Education podcasts	https://itunes.apple.com/us/podcast/istes -podcast/id269480016?mt=2

Figure 5.12: *A list of podcasts for literacy coaches*

TED Talks are influential videos from expert speakers on education, business, science, technology, and creativity. These short, inspirational videos are not only perfect for our own continued learning but for use in our sessions with teachers as well. Through these, we can connect with major researchers and authors and collect inspiring resources for our own work. Figure 5.13 lists a few TED Talks not to be missed.

Although your first inclination might be to focus on education and education-related resources, think outside the box. Go ahead and watch that video about fashion design or microbiology and fuel your curiosity and need for inquiry.

7. Get involved in Edcamps. Edcamps are free events developed by educators for educators. With no plan other than to share our teaching practices and learn from each other, educators gather together and create an agenda for their learning. Scan the QR code to link to ASCD's article on Edcamps and how teachers are taking back their own professional development.

 Scan the QR code to read more about Edcamps.
http://bit.ly/1rWDhlA

Don't have an Edcamp nearby? Don't worry, there are virtual options as well, such as the Annual #EdCampVoxer event. In true Edcamp fashion, participants join Voxer rooms that speak to their own interests and needs to connect with other like-minded administrators, leaders, coaches, and teachers.

 Scan the QR code to read more about virtual Edcamps!
http://bit.ly/2jqKDRQ

TED TALKS	
TED Talks from Inspiring Teachers	www.ted.com/playlists/182/talks_from_inspiring _teachers
Teach Thought's Top 50 TED Talks	www.teachthought.com/pedagogy/50-inspiring-ted -talks-teachers-challenge-eduspective/
Edudemic's 10 Best TED Talks	www.edudemic.com/10-best-ted-talks-of-2014-for -educators/

Figure 5.13: *A list of TED Talks for literacy coaches*

Stay Connected

In most schools, there is a single literacy coach charged with the task to lead the learning of every teacher in the building, which at times can feel isolating. Yet, when we think carefully about the many, varied connections we have with others, we are often surprised to realize that it is such a small world after all, particularly once we connect with technology. Connections exist everywhere on all different levels and we can easily find them—if we simply seek them out. By making the conscious choice to connect with others for the sake of our own professional learning, we expand what is possible. Seek out other coaches who are using digital tools in their coaching and connect together. Here are a few ways to stay connected as you continue in your journey.

1. Stay connected through social media. Create and cultivate professional profiles to remain in touch with others. In Chapter 2, I provided a listing of literacy professionals to follow and chats to participate in. Commit to your social media profile and remain active online. In these moments of connection, collaboration is born.

2. Get involved in professional organizations. At this moment, you are probably a member of the International Literacy Association and/or the National Council of Teachers of English, premier organizations for our work as literacy coaches. Yet, you might also consider joining other organizations specially focused on infusing technology into our coaching and instructions, such as the International Society for Technology in Education. These organizations are specifically focused on bringing technology into our work and can inspire innovations.

3. Expand your virtual learning network. Although social media is powerful, there are other communities that you might become a part of to fuel your learning as well. These communities are made specially of literacy coaches, literacy leaders, and those leading the way in teaching with digital tools and technology. Figure 5.14 offers a few digital and virtual communities you might be interested in.

Technology seems to move at the speed of light. There is always something new, something shiny, and something exciting on the horizon. Even as I wrote this book, I feared that by the time I finished, some of the tools I mention would be obsolete. That still may be true, but if we focus on the pedagogy, not the tool, then our work endures.

COMMUNITIES	
NCTE Village	http://village.ncte.org
edWeb	http://home.edweb.net
International Society for Technology in Education Teacher Education Network	https://plus.google.com/u/0/communities/100106676856576705132
International Literacy Association Special Interest Groups	http://literacyworldwide.org/get-involved/ila-network/special-interest-groups
Literacy in Learning Exchange	http://www2.ncte.org/blog/2015/09/the-literacy-in-learning-exchange/

Figure 5.14: *A list of digital and virtual communities for literacy coaches*

When I was a little girl, I used to have a suitcase labeled with the slogan "Half the fun is getting there." I encourage you to hold onto this idea as you move forward in your coaching journey. We all want a vision of what our transformed coaching might look like, but half the fun, and all the learning, happens in the process of doing so. Embrace the journey ahead, seek out others to connect with and fuel your work, and reap the benefits of coaching in a more connected world through technology.

Onward!

Appendices

To download full-size versions of the Appendices, please visit **http://hein.pub/LiteracyCoaching** and click on the Companion Resources tab.

APPENDIX A — **Literacy Coaching Vision Plan**

Coaching Partnership: _____

GOAL: *What is your instructional focus?*		
PROCESS: *What kind of coaching will best meet your goal?* • *Demonstration?* • *Coteaching?* • *Observation?* • *Combination?*	*What will the teacher do?*	*What will the coach do?*
	What resources are needed?	
LOGISTICS: *What time and tasks are needed to be successful?*	*Precoaching conversation:*	
	Classroom coaching:	
	Postcoaching conversation:	
	Classroom coverage?	
NOTES, OBSERVATIONS, AND QUESTIONS:		

APPENDIX B — **Demonstration Lesson Plan**

Coaching Partnership: _____

Lesson Date: _____

GOAL: *What is your instructional focus?*	
STUDENTS: • *Grade* • *Background* • *Curriculum* • *Rules and routines*	
LESSON: • *Introduction* • *Explicit teaching* • *Guided teaching* • *Independent practice*	
MATERIALS AND RESOURCES: • *Books?* • *Charts and markers?* • *Student materials?*	
THINGS TO THINK ABOUT: • *What else do we need to consider?* • *What artifacts of learning might we reflect on?*	

APPENDIX C — Coteaching Lesson Plan

Coaching Partnership: _____

Lesson Date: _____

GOAL: *What is our instructional focus?*	
STUDENTS: • *Grade* • *Background* • *Curriculum* • *Rules and routines*	

	Lesson Component	Teacher/Coach Roles
LESSON: • *Introduction* • *Explicit teaching* • *Guided teaching* • *Independent practice*		

MATERIALS AND RESOURCES: • *Books?* • *Charts and markers?* • *Student materials?*	
THINGS TO THINK ABOUT: • *What else do we need to consider?* • *What artifacts of learning might we reflect on?*	

APPENDIX D — Literacy Coaching Observation Notes

Classroom Environment		
LOOK FOR: • *Routines* • *Groupings* • *Culture of reading* • *Access to text* • *Materials and resources*	*I notice:*	*I wonder:*
Student Engagement		
LOOK FOR: • *Active engagement* • *Varied methods* • *Teaching tools available?* • *Balance of teacher/student talk*	*I notice:*	*I wonder:*
Literacy Instruction		
LOOK FOR: • *Balanced literacy framework* • *Responsive instruction* • *Differentiation* • *Teacher language* • *Pacing* • *Materials* • *Assessment*	*I notice:*	*I wonder:*
Literacy Content		
LOOK FOR: • *Skills taught and reinforced* • *Strategies taught and reinforced* • *Alignment of instructional language* • *Appropriate text levels*	*I notice:*	*I wonder:*

APPENDIX E —— Literacy Coaching Conversation

Coaching Partnership: _____

CELEBRATIONS: *What went well?*	
INQUIRY: • *What did we wonder about?* • *What do we need to consider?* • *What did not feel quite right?*	
STUDENT RESPONSES AND ARTIFACTS OF LEARNING: • *How did students respond?* • *How do we know?* • *What additional supports are needed?*	
NEXT STEPS: • *Revise goals, process, and logistics.* • *What did we learn about literacy teaching?* • *Where could we head next?* • *What do we need?*	

APPENDIX F — Tech Notes

CHAPTER 2 TECH NOTES				
Tool	Description	Website	Cost	Techspert Level
Goodreads	A site for readers and book recommendations	www.goodreads.com	Free!	Great for beginning tech users
Padlet	A virtual bulletin board	https://padlet.com	Free! Premium plans vary.	Great for beginning tech users
QR Stuff	A QR code generator	www.qrstuff.com	Free! Premium plans vary.	Great for beginning tech users
Google+ Community	An online community discussion board	https://plus.google.com/communities	Free!	Great for beginning tech users
Facebook	Online social networking site	http://facebook.com	Free!	Great for beginning tech users
Voxer	A mobile messaging app	http://voxer.com	Free! Premium plans vary.	Good for users with some tech knowledge
Twitter	Online social networking site	http://twitter.com	Free!	Good for users with some tech knowledge
Bloglovin'	Curates multiple blogs into one feed	www.bloglovin.com	Free!	Great for beginning tech users

CHAPTER 3 TECH NOTES				
Tool	Description	Website	Cost	Techspert Level
Google Forms	A tool to create and analyze surveys	www.google.com/forms/about	Free!	Great for beginning tech users
Flipgrid	A video discussion tool	https://info.flipgrid.com	Free! Premium plans vary.	Great for beginning tech users
TodaysMeet	A back channel for conversation	https://todaysmeet.com	Free!	Great for beginning tech users
Screen-cast-O-Matic	Online screencasting tool	https://screencast-o-matic.com	Free! Premium plans vary.	Great for beginning tech users
Educreations	A recordable, interactive whiteboard	www.educreations.com	Free! Premium plans vary.	Good for users with some tech knowledge

Tool	Description	Website	Cost	Techspert Level
CHAPTER 3 TECH NOTES *(continued)*				
Explain Everything	Collaborative interactive whiteboard app	https://explaineverything.com	Premium plans vary, starts at $24.99.	Good for users with some tech knowledge
AudioBoom	A tool to record and share content online	https://audioboom.com	Free!	Great for beginning tech users
Vocaroo	Online voice recording service	http://vocaroo.com	Free!	Great for beginning tech users
ThingLink	A tool to annotate videos and images	www.thinglink.com	Free! Premium plans vary.	Best for advanced tech users
Diigo	A social bookmarking website	www.diigo.com	Free! Premium plans vary.	Great for beginning tech users
Symbaloo	A social bookmarking site	www.symbaloo.com	Free!	Great for beginning tech users
Pinterest	A social networking site through virtual bulletin boards	www.pinterest.com	Free!	Great for beginning tech users
Google Docs	A tool to collaboratively create Web-based documents	https://docs.google.com	Free!	Great for beginning tech users
CHAPTER 4 TECH NOTES				
Tool	**Description**	**Website**	**Cost**	**Techspert Level**
Google Drive	Cloud storage and backup	www.google.com/drive/	Free!	Great for beginning tech users
Seesaw Learning Journal	A digital portfolio	https://web.seesaw.me/	Free! Premium plans vary.	Great for beginning tech users
Acclaim	A platform to create, annotate, and share videos	www.getacclaim.com/	Premium plans vary.	Good for users with some tech knowledge

References

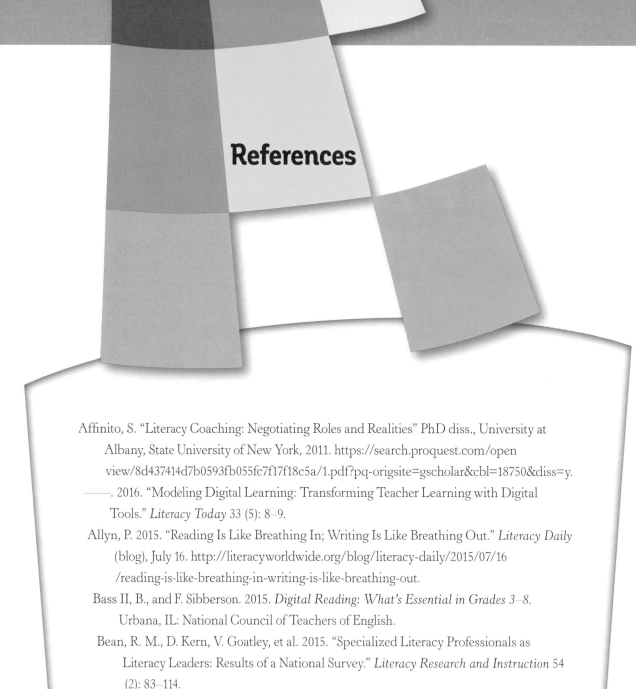

Affinito, S. "Literacy Coaching: Negotiating Roles and Realities" PhD diss., University at
   Albany, State University of New York, 2011. https://search.proquest.com/open
   view/8d437414d7b0593fb055fc7f17f18c5a/1.pdf?pq-origsite=gscholar&cbl=18750&diss=y.
———. 2016. "Modeling Digital Learning: Transforming Teacher Learning with Digital
   Tools." *Literacy Today* 33 (5): 8–9.
Allyn, P. 2015. "Reading Is Like Breathing In; Writing Is Like Breathing Out." *Literacy Daily*
   (blog), July 16. http://literacyworldwide.org/blog/literacy-daily/2015/07/16
   /reading-is-like-breathing-in-writing-is-like-breathing-out.
Bass II, B., and F. Sibberson. 2015. *Digital Reading: What's Essential in Grades 3–8.*
   Urbana, IL: National Council of Teachers of English.
Bean, R. M., D. Kern, V. Goatley, et al. 2015. "Specialized Literacy Professionals as
   Literacy Leaders: Results of a National Survey." *Literacy Research and Instruction* 54
   (2): 83–114.
Burkins, J. M. 2007. *Coaching for Balance: How to Meet the Challenges of Literacy
   Coaching.* Newark, DE: International Reading Association.
Calkins, L., M. Ehrenworth, and C. Lehman. 2012. *Pathways to the Common Core:
   Accelerating Achievement.* Portsmouth, NH: Heinemann.

Casey, K. 2006. *Literacy Coaching: The Essentials.* Portsmouth, NH: Heinemann.

Coiro, J. 2015. "The Magic of Wondering: Building Understanding Through Online Inquiry." *The Reading Teacher* 69 (2): 189–93.

Cole, A., and J. G. Knowles. 2000. *Researching Teaching: Exploring Teacher Development through Reflexive Inquiry.* Boston: Allyn and Bacon.

Common Sense Education. 2015. "Our K–12 Digital Citizenship Curriculum." www.common sensemedia.org/sites/default/files/uploads/classroom_curriculum/cs_digitalcitizenship curric_2016_release.pdf.

Crowley, B. 2014. "3 Steps for Building a Professional Learning Network." http://mobile.edweek .org/c.jsp?cid=25919971&bcid=25919971&rssid=25919961&item=http%3A%2F%2Fapi .edweek.org%2Fv1%2Ftm%2F%3Fuuid%3D0D22F39C-9105-11E4-836E-DBAAB3743667.

#cyberPD Google+ Community. 2016. https://plus.google.com/u/0/communities /107711243109928665922.

Darling-Hammond, L. 2006. *Powerful Teacher Education: Lessons from Exemplary Programs.* San Francisco, CA: Jossey-Bass.

Darling-Hammond, L., and J. Bransford, eds. 2005. *Preparing Teachers for a Changing World: What Teachers Should Learn and Be Able to Do.* San Francisco, CA: Jossey-Bass.

Dole, J. A. 2004. "The Changing Role of the Reading Specialist in School Reform." *The Reading Teacher* 57 (5): 462–72.

Dozier, C. 2006. *Responsive Literacy Coaching: Tools for Creating and Sustaining Purposeful Change.* Portland, ME: Stenhouse.

———. 2008. "Literacy Coaching: Engaging and Learning with Teachers." *The Language and Literacy Spectrum* (18): 11–18.

Dozier, C., P. Johnston, and R. Rogers. 2006. *Critical Literacy, Critical Teaching: Tools for Preparing Responsive Teachers.* New York: Teachers College Press.

Hale, K. 2015. "ISTE 2016 Ignites: Personalize Learning and Empower Students to Change Their Stories" [video]. www.youtube.com/watch?v=tHQ_smL5g6k.

Harvey, S., and H. Daniels. 2009. *Comprehension and Collaboration: Inquiry Circles in Action.* Portsmouth, NH: Heinemann.

Henkes, K. 2013. *The Year of Billy Miller.* New York: HarperCollins.

International Literacy Association. 2015. "Position Statement: The Multiple Roles of School-Based Specialized Literacy Professionals." www.literacyworldwide.org/docs/default-source /where-we-stand/literacy-professionals-position-statement.pdf?sfvrsn=f33aa28e_4.

———. 2016. "Mission Statement." www.literacyworldwide.org.

———. 2017. "Research Brief: The Multiple Roles of School-Based Specialized Literacy Professionals." http://literacyworldwide.org/docs/default-source/where-we-stand/ila-literacy-professionals-research-brief.pdf.

International Reading Association. 2004. "The Role and Qualifications of the Reading Coach in the United States." www.literacyworldwide.org/docs/default-source/where-we-stand/reading-coach-position-statement.pdf?sf.

———. 2009. "New Literacies and 21st-Century Technologies." www.literacyworldwide.org/docs/default-source/where-we-stand/new-literacies-21st-century-position-statement.pdf?sfvrsn=6.

———. 2010. "Standards for Reading Professionals." www.literacyworldwide.org/get-resources/standards/standards-for-reading-professionals.

International Society for Technology in Education. 2016. "ISTE Standards." www.iste.org/standards.

Ippolito, J. 2008. "Exploring Literacy Coaches' Understanding of Responsive and Directive Relationships with Teachers." Prepared for the National Reading Conference. www.researchgate.net/publication/265524338_Responsive_Directive_Coaching_1_Exploring_Literacy_Coaches'_Understanding_of_Responsive_and_Directive_Relationships_with_Teachers.

Kaback, S. 2008. "The Draw-a-Reader Test: Informal Assessment Supporting Teacher Inquiry." www.choiceliteracy.com/articles-detail-view.php?id=391.

Killion, J. 2008. "Are You Coaching Heavy or Light?" *Teachers Teaching Teachers* 3 (8): 1–4.

Lehman, Christopher, and Kate Roberts. 2013. *Falling in Love with Close Reading: Lessons for Analyzing Texts—and Life*. Portsmouth, NH: Heinemann.

Lieberman, A. 1994. "Teacher Development: Commitment and Challenge." In *Teacher Development and the Struggle for Authenticity: Professional Growth and Restructuring in the Context of Change*, edited by P. P. Grimmett and J. Neufeld. New York: Teachers College Press.

Lockwood, J. R., J. S. McCombs, and J. Marsh. 2010. "Linking Reading Coaches and Student Achievement: Evidence from Florida Middle Schools." *Educational Evaluation and Policy Analysis* 32: 372–88.

Lyons, C. A., and G. S. Pinnell. 2001. *Systems for Change in Literacy Education: A Guide to Professional Development*. Portsmouth, NH: Heinemann.

Merriam-Webster Dictionary. 2017. Transform. www.merriam-webster.com/dictionary/transform?utm_campaign=sd&utm_medium=serp&utm_source=jsonld.

Moran, M. C. 2007. *Differentiated Literacy Coaching: Scaffolding for Student and Teacher Success.* Alexandria, VA: Association for Supervision and Curriculum Development.

Muhtaris, K., and K. Ziemke. 2015. *Amplify: Digital Teaching and Learning in the K–6 Classroom.* Portsmouth, NH: Heinemann.

National Center for Literacy Education. 2013. "Remodeling Literacy Learning: Making Room for what Works." www.ncte.org/ncle/2013-report.

———. 2014. "Remodeling Literacy Learning Together: Paths to Standards Implementation." www.ncte.org/library/NCTEFiles/NCLE/2014-NCLE-Report.pdf.

National Council for Teachers of English. 2010. "Teacher Learning Communities." www.ncte.org/library/NCTEFiles/Resources/Journals/CC/0202-nov2010/CC0202Policy.pdf.

———. 2015. "NCTE Framework for 21st Century Curriculum and Assessment." www.ncte.org/positions/statements/21stcentframework.

Rainville, K. N., and S. Jones. 2008. "Situated Identities: Power and Positioning in the Work of a Literacy Coach." *The Reading Teacher* 61 (6): 440–48.

Rami, M. 2014. *Thrive: 5 Ways to (Re)invigorate Your Teaching.* Portsmouth, NH: Heinemann.

Ribble, M. 2008/2009. "Passport to Digital Citizenship: Journey Toward Appropriate Technology Use at School and at Home." *Leading and Learning with Technology* 36 (4): 14–17.

Roberts, K., and M. Beattie Roberts. 2016. *Teaching Tools for Differentiation, Rigor, and Independence.* Portsmouth, NH: Heinemann.

Rodgers, A., and E. M. Rodgers. 2007. *The Effective Literacy Coach: Using Inquiry to Support Teaching and Learning.* New York: Teachers College Press.

Serafini, F. 2015. *Reading Workshop 2.0: Supporting Readers in the Digital Age.* Portsmouth, NH: Heinemann.

Serafini, F., and S. Youngs. 2013. "Reading Workshop 2.0: Children's Literature in the Digital Age." *The Reading Teacher* 66 (5): 401–404.

Serravallo, J. 2015. *The Reading Strategies Book: Your Everything Guide to Developing Skilled Readers.* Portsmouth, NH: Heinemann.

Shulman, L. S., and J. H. Shulman. 2004. "How and What Teachers Learn: A Shifting Perspective." *Journal of Curriculum Studies* 36 (2): 257–71.

Skerrett, A. 2010. "'There's Going to Be Community. There's Going to Be Knowledge': Designs for Learning in a Standardized Age." *Teaching and Teacher Education* 26: 648.

Smith, A. T. 2009. "Considering Literacy Coaching Responsibilities in Terms of Teacher Change." *Literacy Coaching Clearinghouse.* http://literacycoachingonline.org/briefs/coaching_trajectory_a_smith.pdf.

Snow, C., P. Griffin, and S. Burns, eds. 2005. *Knowledge to Support the Teaching of Reading.* San Francisco, CA: John Wiley.

Toll, C. A. 2005. *The Literacy Coach's Survival Guide.* Newark, DE: The International Reading Association.

Vasquez, V. 2010. "iPods, Puppy Dogs and Podcasts: Imagining Literacy Instruction for the 21st century." *School Talk* 15 (2): 1–4.

Walpole, S., and K. L. Blamey. 2008. "Elementary Literacy Coaches: The Reality of Dual Roles." *The Reading Teacher* 62 (3): 222–31.

Walpole, S., and M. C. McKenna. 2008. "Everything You've Always Wanted to Know About Literacy Coaching but Were Afraid to Ask: A Review of Policy and Research." Prepared for the National Reading Conference. www.literacyresearchassociation.org/assets/docs /ConferencePrograms/lra_ann08_onsiteprogram.pdf.

Wise, J. B., and M. Rishel. 2016. "Collaborating in Google Drive to Grow an Instructional Framework for Literacy." *Literacy Daily* (blog). https://literacyworldwide.org/blog /literacy-daily/2016/04/01/collaborating-in-google-drive-to-grow-an-instructional -framework-for-literacy.

Wonderopolis. 2017. Wonder of the Day. https://wonderopolis.org/.